Presented To

St. Mary's
College of Maryland
Library

By _Mrs. Theron A. Thompkins_

Date _April 1967_

In Memory Of

Florence A. Bounds

Authors

of

Liberty

JOHN COLEMAN

Authors of Liberty

Illustrated by C. Edward Beach

VANTAGE PRESS   NEW YORK

WASHINGTON   CHICAGO   HOLLYWOOD

PREFACE

If heroic deeds can consecrate a spot of earth, if the living be still sensible of the example of the dead, if courage be yet a common virtue, and patience in suffering be still honorable; if freedom be any longer precious and faith in humanity be not banished from among you; if love of country still finds a refuge among the hearts of men, "take your shoes from off your feet, for the place on which you stand is holy ground."

HENRY ARMITT BROWN (1878)

Americans may have long been indifferent about their national monuments, their shrines and historic sites; but as the nation comes of age we are mending our mistakes and retrieving many of our long-neglected glories—thanks to the zeal and enterprise of patriotic men and women, historic preservations undertaken on a national scale, the Garden Clubs of America, and other civic bodies. For as much as Americans live by change, they still like to linger over their bygone times and triumphs, and in the shadows of the holy places give thanks and take inspiration. Indeed, the citizens of no country need a better understanding of their past than do we Americans; no country has a story better worth reading than America's.

The richest sources of our heritage are to be found in our shrines and monuments and memorials which Americans are visiting in ever-increasing numbers. All across the nation, these historic landmarks are being snatched from oblivion and restored to their former glory—projects of lasting significance and service.

9

The *Quarterly* of the National Trust for Historic Preservations reminds us that instead of our being fastidious in our application of the term "shrine," the appellation is becoming overworked and often abused: "It is in the extension of its meaning as 'a place or object hallowed from its associations' that overzealous preservationists are making meaningless a word of cherished and explicit meaning. The National Park Service and the Advisory Board on National Parks, Historic Sites, Buildings and Monuments both oppose the casual designation of such areas, which can only weaken the integrity of the truly qualified ones and the criteria by which they are judged. A random selection from the clipping file reveals many proposals for restoration projects in various areas, some having a degree of merit as embodying a significant phase of local history, but frightening when the designation of 'national shrine' is applied."

The distinguished list of restorations and newly erected memorials is constantly augmenting the already-impressive roster of historic sites, reviving for our edification and reflection all our yesterdays, and confirming the promise of Isaiah the prophet: "And they shall build the old wastes, they shall raise up the former desolation." (61:4)

This wistful turning back is something more than sentiment; what we cherish are symbols of hardship and heroism, of devotion and dedication; signposts of progress, milestones of achievement, reminders of an ennobling past. As we relive these yesterdays, reconstruct the scenes and bring alive the personalities which have so enriched our lives, keeping bright memories of kindly things, might we not do well to reflect upon the blessings of liberty which have come down to us through the past? As Henry George wrote in *Progress and Poverty* (1879) "What Liberty shall do for the nation which fully accepts and loyally cherishes her! The wondrous inventions, which are the marked features of this century, give us but a hint. Who is Liberty that we should doubt her or set bounds to her? Is she not peace? Is she not prosperity? Nay, is she not the goal towards which all progress strives?"

Americans in their intelligent travels are thus retrieving from time's crushing flight the greatness of our past, appraising anew our freedom, and reveling in the drama and beauty and making of America. These hallowed places are living reminders of our certain destiny and deeds of glory sometimes forgotten; they are markers of the last visual stand of history.

It is true that Americans who visit other lands will discover mountains far higher, rivers mightier and longer, arts and labors more numerous and more ancient. However, the people of no other nation possess so varied and conclusive a combination of these natural and historical heritages. The years roll on. Ever greater numbers of people will find benefit to body and spirit in these shrines of nature and history; it is beyond the mind of man to measure the essences that are the heritage of every American.

FAIRFIELD OSBORN, in his Prologue to
A Contribution to the Heritage of Every American
by Nancy Newhall; Alfred A. Knopf, 1957.

ACKNOWLEDGMENTS

Thanks are due to the following publishers for permission to quote from publications listed below:

APPLETON-CENTURY-CROFTS, INC.
Circus: From Rome to Ringling by Marian Murray
America Learns to Play by Foster Rhea Dulles

THOMAS Y. CROWELL CO.
Profile of America, edited by Emily Davie. Copyright, 1954 by Emily Davie. Studio Publications, Inc., Thomas Y. Crowell Co., New York, publishers

DOUBLEDAY & CO.
From: *An Almanac of Liberty* by Justice William O. Douglas
Copyright 1954 by William O. Douglas
Reprinted by permission of Doubleday & Co., Inc.
From: *The Great Man* by Howard Swiggett
Copyright 1953 by Howard Swiggett
Reprinted by permission of Doubleday & Co., Inc.
From: *America's National Parks* by Nelson Beecher Keyes
From: *An Introduction to Birds* by John Kieran
Garden City books
Reprinted by permission of Doubleday & Co., Inc.

FUNK & WAGNALLS CO.
Our Wildlife Legacy by Durward L. Allen

HARCOURT, BRACE & CO.
America at Mid-Century by Andre Siegfried

HARPER & BROTHERS
Living Ideas in America by Henry Steele Commager
Far Western Frontier: 1830-1860 by Ray Allen Billington
Politics of Woodrow Wilson, edited by August Heckscher
Profiles in Courage by John F. Kennedy

SIMON AND SCHUSTER, INC.
  Diary of America by Josef and Dorothy Berger
  Why Not Survive? by Michael W. Straus
  My Country by Russell W. Davenport
WM. H. WISE & CO., INC.
  From: Donald H. Sheehan, *This Is My Country*
  By permission of Wm. H. Wise & Co., Inc., publishers

THE QUOTATION

Poor indeed is the man whose mind is not enriched by some phrase of lasting truth and beauty which serves to restore his soul in the exigencies of life. Each of us needs in his heart's treasury the memory of a lovely line to renew fellowship with the great and noble of this earth—and, indeed, almost as great as the ability to use that line to higher levels of emotion and achievement. Here are words of wisdom and thoughts of comfort for all mankind.

From *Leaves of Gold,* edited by Clyde Francis Lytle; Coslett Publishing Co., 1957.

In these informal papers, designed to "lift the fascinating story of America from its musty archives and make it live again so that Americans may better sense their past and understand their present," the quotation has been freely employed because no other medium can lend such graceful and emphatic expression to the American theme. Indeed, it is good for us that the journeyman observer and interpreter has at his command such a well of authoritative knowledge to tap in his quest for the real meaning of America.

For writing is a symphony of words and of research and of reflection and verbal grace—and the unashamed recourse to the quotation, the last of which brings to countless people one of the real joys of the printed page. Indeed, how else could there have been preserved "what is on the tongue, in the heart, in the head; the men, the manners, the events; the smells, the sights, the sounds, of all the years of our being"? It's the quotation that illuminates history. And even through the quoted word, might not men's minds, under the inspiration of Divine Providence, be turned from pillage and slaughter and tyranny toward sanity and succor and good will?

There is a kind of dread on the part of modern writers to employ the quotation by way of pointing up a topic, introducing historic passages of unusual eloquence, lest the misunderstood "average man" be unable to grasp its significance. That misconception, of course, is the very negation of democratic thinking; it is the withholding of "the right to belong." Are we not too prone to underestimate the intellectual capacity of the much-maligned "average man," who is eager to extend his reach and grasp, even as you and I? If a tenet, or a philosophy, or a thing of beauty, or an inspiration, can be best expressed in an historical utterance or in descriptive eloquence finer than one's own, why should a writer cling to mediocrity on the smug assumption that the reader is not capable of rising to a new plateau of literary appreciation?

There has recently been published in Tokyo the *Kenkyusha Dictionary of English Quotations,* which attempts to show by example the use which has been made by modern authors of well-known passages of prose and verse, ranging from the eighteenth century to the present. Of the more than ten thousand instances cited, the ones most frequently quoted were from the Bible—chiefly from the Book of Genesis and the Psalms; Shakespeare—mostly from *Hamlet, Macbeth,* and *Othello;* Milton, Wordsworth, Tennyson, Pope, Shelley; followed by a thousand miscellaneous other sources. The editors found the use of quotation to be much more common among English than among American writers. Contemporory Americans, though resorting to the quotation in their titles, are otherwise inclined to avoid it in their texts.

I suggest that we raise our sights and citations, that we stop feeling inferior because by chance we possess superior knowledge. The man who leans upon John Milton is no more infirm than the man who leans upon

Bob Hope. Our speech is not so rich that we can afford to quote only each other. Current income cannot maintain our linguistic economy—at least in the style to which she is accustomed. The quotation used to make our own speech gayer, our thought clearer does not constrict or paralyse the language. On the contrary it enlarges it, gives it more scope and freedom. At the same time it surreptitiously infuses into our speech—now in peril of subsiding to a prairie flatness relieved only by the tumescences of current slang—a needed elegance, even splendor.

Any Number Can Play, Clifton Fadiman;
World Publishing Company, 1957.

It is a good thing for an uneducated man—and who amongst us is not uneducated—to read and ponder the apt quotation. Engraved upon the memory, it leaves you with good thoughts; and it makes you anxious to read the author and to look for more.

WINSTON CHURCHILL

The American is the hope of the human race. He may become the model. He ought to show the world by facts, that men can be free and yet peaceful, and may dispense with the chains in which tyrants and knaves of every color have presumed to bind them, under pretext of the public good. The Americans should be an example of political, religious, commercial and industrial liberty. The asylum they offer to the oppressed of every nation, the avenue of escape they open, will compel governments to be just and enlightened; and the rest of the world in due time will see through the empty illusions in which policy is conceived. But to obtain these ends for us, America must secure them to herself.

ANNE ROBERT JACQUES TURGOT;
French statesman and economist; 1727-1781.

CONTENTS

INTRODUCTION

HERE is America as revealed by our national shrines, sanctuaries, monuments and memorials; here is history as written in early American episodes—the roots from which our country sprang. These pages pin down the past for us in the inspiration and words of both statesmen and plain people—words that bring into bold relief the nation's progress, set the guideposts for the daily concerns of the present, and have recourse to Divine Providence in directing our lives and fortunes.

Designed to revive a neglected pride in our courage and aspirations and culture, the material richness of our lives, the spiritual hopes of our hearts, these pages extol our heritage of sites and scenes and sentiments—the testaments to which we may turn for steadfastness and faith when we are beset with doubts and fears.

J.C.

Authors

of

Liberty

THE FIRST AMERICANS

Up to 1880 the country through which the Little Missouri flows remained as wild and almost as unknown as it was when the old explorers and fur traders found it in the early part of the century. It was the last great Indian hunting ground, across which Grosventres and Mandans, Sioux and Cheyennes and even Crows and Rees wandered in chase of game and where they fought one another and plundered the small parties of white trappers and hunters that occasionally ventured into it.

> *Theodore Roosevelt's America,* edited by
> Farida A. Wiley; American Naturalists Series;
> Devin-Adair Co.

What is heralded as the largest memorial monument in the world is being projected as a tardy tribute to the original American—the North American Indian. By joint congressional resolution, there is to be erected a permanent shrine around the heroic figure of the Indian chieftain, Crazy Horse, chiseled out of Thunder Head Mountain in the

Black Hills of South Dakota by the eminent sculptor Ziol-kowski.

A boulevard to run along the mountain-side would be lined with rock-hewn figures of other great Indian leaders. The plan also calls for a museum, as well as a medical research center for the study of health problems of the various tribes. The pretentious design would dwarf even the colossal carvings of Washington, Jefferson, Lincoln, and Theodore Roosevelt on neighboring Mount Rushmore.

Thus the Crazy Horse Memorial Foundation will preserve and perpetuate the history and culture of the American Indian.

It has been generally recognized that these Red Men of the plains and the pueblos, while primarily men of action and inured to hardship which they willingly accepted, had a deep spiritual side and a fine respect for that inner life so often neglected by their more "civilized" brothers. This inner life meant so much to them, as one historian has observed, that they endured what would be to us almost incredible physical ordeals in the hope of becoming the kind of men they wanted most to be.

After a decade of intermittent skirmishes and wars with the white men—even bloody massacres—encroachments in 1875 upon the sacred stronghold of the Sioux precipitated the desperate battle of the Rosebud.

With their resourceful warrior, Crazy Horse, the Indians of the plains were a superb light cavalry whose main subsistence had been the buffalo herds which were being wantonly decimated by white marauders. Friction with ranchers, gold-rush miners, and homesteaders further aggravated relations, as did exploitation by unscrupulous Indian agents and the opening of the West by the Northern Pacific Railway.

American troops were forced to fall back, and the Indians proceeded toward the Big Horn Mountains to replenish their ammunition and buffalo rations. Meanwhile Lt. Col. George A. Custer was dispatched to intercept them—it was to be the famed Custer's last stand. A force of twenty-five

hundred Sioux under Sitting Bull fell upon him and cut his
force to pieces, not one of the entire detachment of some
two hundred men surviving. The Indians then scattered
and were subsequently rounded up in the mountainous country by troop reinforcements and taken off to other reservations.

Fair recognition of other Indian stalwarts has been long
overdue: some historians of Indian lore and prowess place
Tecumseh, chief of the Shawnee Tribe, in a mold of greater
stature than any of the other warriors. A frontier fighter
before the War of 1812, he threw in his lot with the British and was killed in action at the battle of the Thames.
Despite his antipathy toward the whites, Tecumseh was at
once a considerate and resourceful leader, brilliant but hu-
mane. He possessed those virtues rare in an Indian chieftain
of strict adherence to his pledged word and of a toleration
that had been unknown to his fellows. His most recent and
comprehensive biography, *Tecumseh: Vision of Glory,* by
Glen Tucker, extols "a great statesman whose oratorical
powers and military acumen were matched by his personal
magnetism." The Union commander, William Tecumseh
Sherman, bears his name.

Chief Seattle gives us a penetrating character sketch of the
fast vanishing earliest Americans in his address made before
signing the Treaty of 1885 with the white men: "We are two
distinct races with separate origins and separate destinies.
There is little in common between us. To us the ashes of
our ancestors are sacred and their resting place is hallowed
ground. You wander far from the graves of your ancestors
and seemingly without regret. Your religion was written on
tables of stone by the iron finger of your God so that you
could not forget. The red man could never comprehend nor
remember it. Our religion is the tradition of our ancestors—
the dreams of our old men, given them in the solemn hours
of night by the great spirit, and the visions of our sachem,
and it is written in the hearts of our people.

"Your dead cease to love you and the land of their nativity as soon as they pass the portals of the tomb and wander away beyond the stars. They are soon forgotten and never return. Our dead never forget the beautiful world that gave them being—they still love its verdant valleys, its murmuring rivers, its magnificent mountains, sequestered vales and verdant-lined lakes and bays, and even yearn in tender, fond affection over the lonely hearted living and often return from the happy hunting ground to visit, guide, console and comfort them."

> From *Profile of America—an Autobiography of the U.S.A.* Edited by Emily Davie; Thomas Y. Crowell Co., 1954.

> Where is my home—my forest home?
> The proud land of my sires?
> Where stands the wigwam of my pride?
> Where gleam the council fires?
> Where are my father's hallowed graves?
> My friends so light and free?
> Gone, gone—forever from my view!
> Great Spirit! Can it be?

> SAMUEL G. DRAKE, *Indians of North America,* 1880.

IN THE OLD DOMINION—I

From out of the centuries that are gone have come voices
of great men, which seem still to echo back the prayers
and praises of the past. The Restoration speaks to the
present and the future of what is highest and noblest
in life, recalling the best that the past holds and presenting it as an ideal and inspiration to men, calling very
strongly to them to live for the things that count and
the strength and glory of the nation.

Reverend W. A. R. Goodwin, *What Williamsburg
Means To Me;* Evelyn Goodwin Farr; privately
printed.

Thanks to the inspiration of the late Dr. W. A. R. Goodwin, rector of hallowed Bruten Parish Church, and the mu-
nificence of Mr. John D. Rockefeller, Jr., Virginia's colonial
capital and the early seat of royal governors, has been restored
to its eighteenth-century grace and dignity—a Cinderella city
come to life again, the American shrine of shrines, the great
central masterpiece of Virginia's triple crown—Williams-

23

burg, Mount Vernon, Monticello. More than half a million visitors make the pilgrimage every year, the better to understand what it feels like to be an American: here is live and stirring history, a vital segment of the American past embracing a period of more than three hundred years.

The heroic concept of restoration carried out with such meticulous fidelity has entailed a benefaction of perhaps fifty million dollars. Scattered over 220 acres, some six hundred modern structures were razed, eighty colonial buildings brought back to their original dignity, and hundreds more reconstructed upon their old foundations, every brick drenched in history!

The Palace where the governors held forth, the House of Burgesses—oldest American representative assembly—; Raleigh Tavern, where the gentry joined in debate and revelry and where, according to tradition, students from near-by William and Mary College founded in 1776 the Phi Beta Kappa Society, still a coveted honor; the Wythe House, Washington's headquarters prior to the siege of Yorktown; places of worship; shops and sundry establishments of the crafts—all adjacent to Duke of Gloucester Street, one of early America's noblest thoroughfares. Plays and pageants and concerts enhance the scene, and tours are conducted under the guidance of costumed escorts who explain the origins and recite the glories of the inspiring era. Surrounding the buildings, housing faithful reproductions of the original furnishings and fabrics, formal colonial gardens have sprung up again on their original sites. The Wren building, of world renown, is the oldest academic building standing in this country.

"But the significance of Williamsburg," writes the historian Dumas Malone, author of *Jefferson and His Times* (Little, Brown & Co.), "arose from its *public* character; its enduring meaning lies in the deeds and ideas that are associated with it and in the wonderful public men it nurtured: Washington, Jefferson, George Mason, Edmund Pendleton, George Wythe, Patrick Henry, Richard Henry Lee; and, among the younger patriots, James Madison, James Monroe, John Marshall.

"The implacable hostility of these men to tyranny and their emphasis on freedom," observes Mr. Malone, "are unmistakable. In an era of change these gentlemen-planters who had been schooled in self-government and who viewed privileged position and public responsibility as inseparable, put themselves on record as believing that the rights they claimed for themselves belonged to all men everywhere. This is a glorious fact of history."

And this observation comes from a modern commentator, speaking of a series of forthcoming historical biographies: "For all these great men we now have or soon shall have an incomparable record. Anyone who has the patience will be able to live their lives over with them, step by step, through the successive problems they faced—problems that were often surprisingly similar to our own. To associate with these patriots of Old America is not to escape from reality; it is to come into their reality and to enjoy a memorable personal experience. We may rejoice, therefore, that they are being authentically restored in their full dimensions; and we may hope that Americans increasingly will become conscious of what is truly great in their country's past."

Sir Winston Churchill recently became the first recipient of the Williamsburg Award—a continual reminder that there are today, as there were yesterday, vigorous, courageous, and eloquent leaders who have championed and advanced the basic principles of liberty and justice in the world. Thus by this fresh accolade, Churchill is associated with American patriots who gained their first fame by disowning a British Parliament and defying a British monarch, "the great Englishman of our times sharing the undying belief in human freedom and the dignity of the individual which was manifest in the greatest of these historic Virginians."

The right emotions for the historian are nostalgia, imagination and humility; he will bridge the gulf between the present and the past with the brisk variety and unexpectedness of life. He can adopt selection and compression—plenty of facts, lots of records, despatches and deeds, private letters and public announcements—choosing those which will make the story clear, arranging them so as to bring out the essentials of historical change.

GILBERT HIGHET, *People, Places and Books;* Oxford University Press, 1953.

History is too important to be a fenced-in preserve for the professional historian. Intellectually curious people, though quite unprofessional, ought to read it, study it, and on occasion write it.

WILLIS THORNTON, *Fable, Fact and History;* Greenberg: 1957.

Williamsburg is made for the prosperous millions, for the "middling sort" of Americans, for a nation of paved roads and automobile owners and well-paid vacations, for a child-centered, newspaper-reading nation where families do things together. It symbolizes the American refusal to segregate any kind of activity: the refusal to believe that education need be a chore, or that learning need be confined to solemn and studious hours. Business and pleasure ought to be combined. Americans like to learn together, they like to enjoy their education. For these purposes Williamsburg is perfectly suited, and in a way which has no parallel.

"Past and Present in America," *Historic Preservation;* National Trust for Historic Preservation, 1958.

THE OLD DOMINION—II

We are a people whose history has made us the land of
the swift, total solution, brought about by ourselves
alone. We faced a wilderness and we hacked it down. We
were vexed by slavery; we cut it out of our system. No
wonder we are the only country in the world which has
produced a popular saying to the effect that "difficult
things we do immediately; the impossible takes a little
time."

> ERIC F. GOLDMAN, *The Crucial Decade;*
> Alfred A. Knopf, 1956.

Other historical spots, almost as compelling as the restored grandeur of Williamsburg, bring history alive elsewhere in the Old Dominion—birthplace of the nation. In
1607 the Indians watched with amazement as Captain John
Smith's armada of *The Susan Constant, Godspeed,* and *Dis-*

covery dropped anchor off the site that became Jamestown, whose complement of adventurers were to establish the first permanent English settlement in America. As the capital of Virginia, known until 1698 as Middle Plantation, celebrates its three-hundred-and-fiftieth anniversary of the landing, St. Luke's Church is being formally opened to the public, restored to its beauty and dignity of three hundred years ago, its box pews, font, bells, pulpit, lectern, and *torchères* duplicating the originals. It stands on its ancient site adjacent to the near-by village of Smithfield.

The battlefield at Yorktown—"where one miracle led to another"—and where Cornwallis surrendered in 1781, did much to assure independence for the Colonies. Now a National Park located on a strip of land between the York and James Rivers in tidewater Virginia, it is a Revolutionary landmark. The Articles of Capitulation were arranged in the Moore house, which still stands on the battlefield. Recently there has been discovered what remains of historic "Redoubt Number 10," key outer defense of the British lines. Capture of this bunker and its companion strongpoint "Number 9" proved to be the turning point in the battle.

Richmond, the capital of the Confederacy, already harboring many sites of historical interest—the Capitol, designed by Thomas Jefferson; Lee House; the Edgar Allen Poe Shrine; the home of Chief Justice John Marshall; old St. John's Church, where Patrick Henry threw out his stirring challenge: "Is life so dear, or peace so sweet, as to be purchased at the price of chains and slavery? Forbid it, Almighty God! I know not what course others may take, but as for me, give me liberty or give me death!" A Hall of Memory honors Virginia's dead of World War II and of the Korean conflict—an imposing structure on whose walls are inscribed the names of 19,642 of Virginia's sons. Arlington House, or Lee Mansion, on the Virginia Heights opposite Washington, where the Custis and Lee families lived before the Civil War, is now a national memorial to the great Confederate leader. At the time of his death in 1870,

Lee had remained ineligible to hold civil or military office and was deprived of certain other rights of citizenship. But a resolution has been proposed to restore these to him because of his "knightly virtues of courage, patriotism and selfless devotion to duty."

Shenandoah National Park, an area of great natural beauty, of battlefields where the nation's course was changed, of gracious mansions of the leaders in the early days of the Republic; Winchester, the scene of many military engagements of the Civil War; Lexington, with its famed Washington and Lee University and Virginia Military Institute, the West Point of the South; and near-by Natural Bridge— one of the seven natural wonders of the world . . . Fredericksburg, where Washington attended school for a time, and where he often visited his mother in the frame house at Charles and Lewis Streets where she spent the last seventeen years of her life . . . Two blocks away is Kenmore, built in 1752 by Fielding Lewis for his bride, Betty, Washington's only sister—a notable example of colonial architecture, restored to its original elegance and furnished with priceless antiques.

Not far away is Wakefield, built on the site of the Washington Plantation residence; the original dwelling in which he was born burned in 1779. The Rising Sun Tavern still stands where Virginia notables were wont to meet to draft parliamentary measures; as does the only home in this country of the naval hero John Paul Jones. For all its varied background and associations, Fredericksburg remains the "Washington town," rich in the history, legends, and memories of America's first family. Alexandria, too, the "seaport" town on the Potomac, is full of Washington associations. Gadsby's Tavern, built in 1752, once served as General Washington's headquarters, and he held his last military review from its front steps.

A new National Monument has been created at Harper's Ferry, on the border of the Old Dominion where it joins West Virginia, the scene of the abortive raid on the Federal arsenal by the abolitionist, John Brown, who sought to incite the slaves into rebellion. He was captured and hanged at Charles Town by Robert E. Lee, then colonel of the United States Cavalry. One of the important places of Virginia a century ago, the ravages of floods and wars reduced it for a while to a ghost town. The land on which it stands has been changed to West Virginia, and a long-term restoration program will perpetuate its old landmarks and historic associations. From a bluff overlooking the junction of the Potomac and Shenandoah Rivers—visited by more than 100,000 people every year—the sightseer obtains a spectacular panorama of three states.

Looking upon the confluence of the two rivers—where a Philadelphia millwright named Robert Harper operated his ferry—Thomas Jefferson, two centuries ago, was moved to indulge his powers of description. "On your right," he wrote, "comes up the Shenandoah, having ranged along the foot of the mountain an hundred miles to seek a vent. On your left approaches the Patowmac, in quest of a passage also. In the moment of their junction they rush together against the mountain, rend it asunder, and pass on to the sea . . . This scene is worth a voyage across the Atlantic. . . ."

It is time for all of us to reacquaint ourselves with our historical treasures and the moral values which inspired our forefathers to lead our country to the pinnacle of world leadership.

The time is opportune to reinform America of the inspiring story of our glorious democratic history of liberty, freedom, tolerance and justice. We must pass on to our young people the greatness that is America's. We must remind all of our citizens of the wealth of our Nation's moral and spiritual treasures. By reflecting upon the glories of our past, we can advance in the future.

J. Edgar Hoover, speaking before the National Convention of the American Legion. Reprinted in *American Mercury* Magazine, January, 1958.

THE LANDINGS

In the name of God, Amen. We whose names are underwritten, having undertaken for the glory of God, and advancement of the Christian Faith, and honor of our king and country, a voyage to plant the first colony in Virginia, do by these presents, solemnly and mutually in the presence of God and one of another, covenant and combine ourselves together into a civil body politic, for our better ordering and preservation; and to enact such just and equal laws as shall be thought most meet and convenient for the general good of the colony, unto which we promise all due submission and obedience.

From *The Mayflower Compact*

Thus to avoid factions and discord among the settlers, there was drawn up the covenant while the *Mayflower* rode at anchor at the site of Provincetown off Cape Cod, Massachusetts, November 11, 1620. Instead of proceeding to a landing place in Virginia, as originally intended, the *Mayflower*, blown off her course, hove to a month later at Plymouth, where a large rock protrudes into the sea, having sailed from Plymouth, England, in September—an odyssey

31

which required more than three months' time at sea. But
the fabled ROCK has gradually become a matter of legend
and hearsay: there appears to be no mention in any of the
authentic accounts of the sea saga that the landing party
first disembarked thereon, probably rowing ashore in the
Mayflower's thirty-foot longboat, or shallop.

> Being thus passed the vast ocean and come to good har-
> bor, the pilgrims found no friends to welcome them, nor
> inns to entertain or refresh their weatherbeaten bodies,
> no houses to repair to for succor. They could see nothing
> but a desolate wilderness, full of wild beasts and wild
> men. If they looked behind them, there was the mighty
> ocean which they had passed, which had now become a
> gulf separating them from all the civil parts of the world.
>   WILLIAM BRADFORD, Governor of Plymouth, the
>   first American historian.

These separatists from the Church of England, joined in
Holland by others, numbered 102 souls, with a crew of some
forty hands. Someone's remark that "they knew they were
pilgrims on a religious journey" led to their being called
"Pilgrims," as distinct from the Puritans of the Massachusetts Bay Colony founded later, in 1630. Half the colonists
perished from cold, hunger, and illness during the ordeal
of the ensuing winter. Nineteen years later, in 1639, they,
together with their Indian friends, celebrated the first
Thanksgiving Day.

The little settlement of Plymouth has since become an
industrial community and summer resort. In 1824, Pilgrim
Hall was established, housing rare paintings, period furniture, the cradle of Peregrine White—the first white child
to be born in the Colonies—the sword of Capt. Miles Stan-
dish, the expedition's military leader, the Bible of Governor Bradford, old letters and manuscripts, church records,
the original patent of the Plymouth Colony—all comprising

an historic collection of the earliest New England Americana—the first New England shrine. Plymouth Town Hall, built in 1749, is the oldest government building still functioning in the United States. There is also the national memorial to the forefathers, said to be the largest granite monument in the world, with its heroic figures representing Faith, Morality, Law, Education, and Freedom.

In addition to their quest for religious liberty, the Pilgrim Fathers brought to our shores the principle of free enterprise and of stock ownership as a form of wealth. Many of the *Mayflower*'s complement were stockholders in the English Plymouth Company, whose shares were then being traded on the London Stock Exchange. The New York Stock Exchange was not formed until 1792, doing business under a buttonwood tree on Wall Street, and a small group of stock issues made their initial trading appearance when the New York *Commercial Advertiser* first published a list of American stocks in its issue of March 10, 1815, the descriptions including for the most part a handful of bank and insurance-company shares. Of the millions of people who today own stock in publicly held United States companies, approximately half the number are women. Indeed, a century ago, one of New York's most patronized brokerage firms consisted of the partnership of Miss Victoria Woodhull and Miss Tennessee Claflin. "All gentlemen will state their business," read the office ultimatum, "and then retire at once." The ladies had their pretty fingers in finance long before they won the right of suffrage!

Another *Mayflower*—the name derives from the blossom of the English hawthorne—a replica, as nearly as could be, of her predecessor which sailed to our shores in 1620, fetched up at Plymouth, Massachusetts, in 1957 after a two-month's sail from the Old World Plymouth in England. While the measurements and exact type of rigging of the original *Mayflower* have been lost to history, her modern counterpart was faithfully fashioned at the two-hundred-year-old Upham

Shipyard in the fishing port of Brixham on the Devon coast. This newest ancient caravel is a 92-footer of about 200 tons' displacement, with ribs of stout English oak, built at a cost of some three hundred thousand dollars raised by popular subscription, and representing a gesture of good will from the people of Great Britain to the people of the United States, plus a generous sprinkling of commercialism!

Except for modern navigating instruments, the twentieth-century "pioneer" was outfitted as of old, and made the crossing entirely under sail, following for the most part the course taken by the seventeenth-century sailors. Her complement consisted of twenty-one crew members and forty male passengers, screened from more than twelve hundred applicants, many of the volunteers for duty having been young girls. Among the ship's company were a number of descendants of the original voyagers. All on board were outfitted in the dress of the period.

At the helm was Commander Alan John Villiers, a distinguished veteran of sailing ships, who has given this commentary on the exploit: "Our re-enactment of that voyage of 337 years ago is much more than a memorial to the imperishable splendor of the faith and courage of the noble and simple men who formed that first band. It recalls one of the heroic achievements of modern history and symbolizes virtues whereof men always stand in need. We are seeking to keep the wonderful ideals of the Pilgrim Fathers alive on both sides of the Atlantic."

The new *Mayflower II*, anchored at Plimoth Plantation, will be on permanent exhibition in Plymouth harbor—another memorial of America's beginnings.

No people who went out to form a colony were ever so ill-trained or so poorly provided with materials to make a success as these. Yet none came through so triumphantly. We may well echo the noble words of Bradford: "Our fathers were Englishmen which came over this great ocean, and were ready to perish in this wilderness;

but they cried unto the Lord, and He heard their voice. Let them therefore praise the Lord, because He is good; and His mercies endure forever."

SAMUEL ELIOT MORISON, *The Story of the "Old Colony" of New Plymouth;* Alfred A. Knopf, 1956.

And from another quarter and in another vein, this commentary upon the Pilgrims by a leading historian of the colonial period:

Their intellectual and material poverty, lack of business enterprise, unfavorable situation and defenseless position in the eyes of the law rendered them almost a negative factor in the later life of New England. No great movement can be traced to their initiation, no great leader to birth within their borders, and no great work of art, literature or scholarship to those who belonged to this unpretending company. The Pilgrim Fathers stand rather as an emblem of virtue than a molding force in the life of the nation.

DR. CHARLES M. ANDREWS, *The Fathers of New England;* Yale University Press, 1921.

THE FORGOTTEN MAN

There is a surge in our history like the surge of the sea, and as blind and powerful. And like the sea, the heavings have often tossed men and events to symbolic peaks as high as Ararat and there left them, to remain for the most part secure and shining in the mellow light of history. The same heavings, too, have tossed other men and events of importance onto remote and obscure shores, then ebbed to leave them as forgotten almost as if they had never lived or occurred—many of them covered with the sand and silt of a hundred years and more.

 STEWART H. HOLBROOK, *Lost Men of American History;* Macmillan, 1948.

It is well that Gunston Hall still stands in Fairfax County, Virginia, to help us keep fresh the memory of George Mason—father of the American Bill of Rights. While his life and works are familiar to scholars and historians, this man who achieved such heroic stature amid the early throes of representative government in America has somehow remained in relative obscurity in the mind of the average citizen. While he belongs in that distinguished company of truly great men, George Mason never thought of himself as being of the elect—a self-effacement which is an essential element of magnanimity. That the world's foremost champion of human liberty and dignity should be reckoned as America's most forgotten man is as he would have had it.

"Those who rise to power—and in power, ride roughshod over the rights of men—seem always to stand in marble on our public squares. Those who carry the torch of freedom are soon forgotten—perhaps to be rediscovered centuries later. The American people are more indebted to George Mason for the liberties they now enjoy than to any other mortal man living or dead."

George Mason was born in 1725 and died in 1792. Characteristically Virginian, he was half practical farmer, half lawyer and classical scholar. Patrick Henry called him the greatest statesman he ever knew; Jefferson spoke of him as a man "of the first order of wisdom among those who acted on the theatre of the Revolution; of expansive mind, sound judgment, cogent in argument."

R. Carter Pittman, prominent Georgia attorney, pays him this tribute, writing in the *Journal* of the National Society of Autograph Collectors:

When George Mason went to Williamsburg in May, 1776, he held something in his pocket that revolutionized a world. His Virginia Bill of Rights was to become the most influential constitutional document ever penned by man. Nothing in all the annals of history had ever approached its simple delineation of the inherent rights of men. In that document man stood forth in dignity and freedom as the natural maker and master of his own government. Many fox holes of liberty reconstructed by Mason's fabulous mind form the bitter struggles of man to achieve liberty and dignity in all ages, and were framed into a governmental structure by his pen for the first

time, thence to re-echo forever down the corridors of
time.

Probably the most powerful weapon that has ever been
devised against dictatorship, the first ten Amendments were
ratified in 1792, and thus became as binding as the Constitution itself—a monumental milestone in American history,
ranking in the forefront of our days of commemoration—and
Gunston Hall, the author's early dwelling place, surviving
as one of the nation's most cherished shrines.

With the annual observance of Bill of Rights Day each
December, our people are reminded that this immortal
document vouchsafes to them their most precious liberties:

Freedom of Speech
Freedom of the Press
Freedom of Religion
The Right to Peaceable Assembly
The Right of Petition to the Government
The Right of Privacy and Freedom from Unreasonable
    Search and Seizure
The Right to a Fair Trial and Protection against Exces-
    sive Punishment
The Right to a Choice of Labor
The Right to Own Property
The Right to Belong
As man gives himself to Faith, to Principle, or to Deeds
    of High Cause

—privileges which are indispensable to our happiness and
security and which reaffirm our belief in the dignity of the
individual.

From the point of view of political philosophy, the two
great questions of the Revolutionary era were how men
make government and how government can be limited.
The men who fought the Revolution and wrote the
American Constitution feared government. They sub-

scribed, in varying degrees, to the aphorism of Tom
Paine that "government, like dress, is the badge of lost
innocence"; and to Jefferson's comparable precept that
"that government was best that governed least." To
them, history had taught one grand lesson—that government was never to be trusted, that all governments
tended to be despotic, and that the highest duty of statesmanship was to prevent government from impairing the
rights of men. When we turn today to such great documents as George Mason's Virginia Bill of Rights, and
that of Massachusetts, drafted almost entirely by John
Adams, we must keep in mind that they were written
and adopted by men who believed in "inalienable"
rights so sacred that no government could infringe on
or impair or deny them. That is a philosophical principle
to which we might well return.

HENRY STEELE COMMAGER, *Living Ideas in America;*
Harper & Bros., 1951.

Another unsung patriot was the Revolutionary political
leader, John Hanson of Maryland, first President of the
Continental Congress, 1781–82, after ratification of Articles
of Confederation. Slighted by history, this zealot in the cause
of liberty played a leading part in enlisting the wavering
state of Maryland in the War of Independence.

"We will win the war with George Washington in the
field," he assured his listeners, "if we do our share at home.
In the end we will establish an Inseparable Union, and ultimately it will become the greatest nation in the world."

In his address on heroes and idealists, Justice Oliver
Wendell Holmes predicted:

Men who never heard of him will be moving to the
measure of his thought.

The ability to think straight, some knowledge of the
past, some vision of the future, some skill to do useful
service—these are the most vital things. If we can achieve

them in the citizens of our land, then we shall have brought to America the wisdom and the courage to match her destiny.

VIRGINIA C. GILDERSLEEVE, *Many a Good Crusade;* Macmillan, 1954.

The supreme purpose of history is a better world. History gives a warning to those who would promote war. History brings inspiration to those who seek peace. In short, history helps us learn. Yesterday's records can keep us from repeating yesterday's mistakes.

HERBERT HOOVER, speaking on his eighty-third birthday.

With the recent issue of a twenty-five cent United States postage stamp, commemorating the 183rd anniversary of the ride of Paul Revere, we are reminded that another night galloper also deserves our homage—Dr. Sam Prescott. Faring forth, "booted and spurred," to warn the countryside of the approach of the British Redcoats, Revere fell among a detachment of British troops at Lexington; but Prescott, luckily, happened to be in town that night paying sly court to "Miss Lexington of 1775." Evading the enemy troops, he pressed on to spread the alarm as far as Concord.

Nor should we forget John Peter Muhlenberg, "the Lutheran pastor-patriot and close friend of Washington, the hero of Brandywine and Germantown, leader in the final assault at Yorktown where he gained undying laurels. His Virginia regiment, composed of old parishioners, was said to be the most zealous and alert." His statue stands in the Capitol at Washington, a tribute from his native Pennsylvania.

The American Historical Scene; University of Pennsylvania Press, 1935.

THE CRUCIBLE

As a native American, I exult in the triumph and truth that the country which gave me birth, is destined, both politically and physically, to be the free asylum for the oppressed and the distressed of the Universal World. As an American, with far more than a million millions of the square acres of my native soil around me, I cannot so far crush my feelings of philanthropy and honest pride as to tell mankind that this wide world affords no asylum for suffering humanity—no refuge for the oppressed. On the contrary, I would tell them that it is here without money and without price, and that we lay claim but to an humble need of beneficence, even for this gratuity; for never had a people so much to give at so slight a sacrifice.

HENRY E. RIELL, *An Appeal To The Voluntary Citizens;* New York, 1840.

That your memorialists, while they presume most respectfully to solicit your attention to the helpless and suffering condition of the numerous foreigners, who, flying from a complicated mass of want and misery, daily seek an asylum in the bosom of the Unted States, are emboldened by the recollection that a liberal encouragement to the settlement of meritorious strangers, has always characterized the government and constituted authorities of this union. The wise and brave fathers and founders of its independence, held out to the oppressed and suffering of every nation the consoling assurance, that in this country, at least, they should find a refuge and a home.

The Memorial of the New York Irish Emigrant Association; Niles' Register, 1818.

Another cornerstone of the American heritage is presently to be laid: The American Museum of Immigration—a national shrine of American ancestry to be erected at the foot of the Statue of Liberty on Bedloe's Island—lately renamed Liberty Island—in New York Harbor. It is altogether fitting that the museum should rise at the base of the beacon of freedom which has, for more than seventy years, beckoned millions from the Old World to our shores. Indeed, the Statue of Liberty itself is a symbol of the friendship between peoples, inasmuch as it was a gift from the citizens of France.

"America is God's crucible. Here you stand in your fifty groups, with your fifty languages and histories, and your fifty blood hatreds and rivalries. But you won't be long like that, brothers, for these are the fires of God you've come to. Germans and Frenchmen, Irishmen and Englishmen, Jews and Russians—into the crucible with you all. God is making the American. The real American has not yet arrived—he will be the fusion of all races, the common superman." (Israel Zangwill, 1864–1926.)

This will be the first suitable base ever designed for the statue; it is an undertaking in which all Americans may share and take great pride, for all Americans, except the Indians, are immigrants. The project will strengthen national unity by telling the story of the making of America by people of all countries, creeds, colors, and cultures of the world—a sanctuary where all Americans may rededicate themselves in a common purpose to our faith in freedom as the keystone of the dignity and destiny of man.

The colossal copper statue, measuring 305 feet from its base to the tip of the torch, is probably the largest ever made, being three times the size of the storied Colossus of Rhodes. Since 1886, Miss Liberty has graced the entrance to New York Harbor when President Grover Cleveland accepted, for the American people, the sculptured goddess— the work of Frédéric Auguste Bartholdi, assisted by Gustave Eiffel, creator of the Eiffel Tower. The torch held aloft in her right hand—her left hand grasps a tablet representing the Declaration of Independence—summons the dispossessed of foreign lands to fresh opportunity here in America, promising liberation from tyranny and persecution.

Engraved on a tablet at the main entrance of the pedestal, Emma Lazarus' poem, "The New Colossus," keynotes the purpose and aspirations of the symbolic undertaking:

> Not like the brazen giant of Greek fame,
> With conquering limbs astride from land to land,
> Here at our sea-washed, sunset gates shall stand
> A mighty woman with torch, whose flame
> Is the imprisoned lightning, and her name

Mother of exiles, from her beacon-hand
Glow world-wide welcome; her mild eyes command
The air-bridged harbor that twin cities frame,
"Keep ancient lands, your storied pomp," cries she
With silent lips, "Give me your tired, your poor;
Your huddled masses, yearning to breathe free,
The wretched refuse of your teeming shore;
Send these, the homeless, tempest-tost to me,
I lift my lamp beside the golden door!"

The museum will be designed to record the prodigious contribution to America of its foreign-born and its citizens of foreign ancestry. Bearing the enthusiastic endorsement of President Eisenhower, the project will be under the chairmanship of Maj. Gen. Ulysses S. Grant III; Mr. Pierre du Pont III will be chairman of the Executive Committee; the sixth Alexander Hamilton is secretary-treasurer. The trustees make up a roster of distinguished and public-spirited men and women. The museum will belong to every American, because he and his forbears make up the very fabric of America.

It will be built not as a government project but by a nonprofit corporation which is to raise five million dollars through voluntary contributions from Americans from every walk of life as a national expression of gratitude for the blessings of unity and abundance which we enjoy. The National Park Service of the United States Department of the Interior, which is the official custodian of the Statue of Liberty, will administer the museum as an integral part of the Statue of Liberty National Monument. It will be chartered by the Board of Regents of the state of New York; it is planned to record the names of all who lend their support to the endeavor on a plaque at the foot of the statue.

Located within the walls of the old fort which surrounds the base of the statue, the museum will have some 50,000 square feet of space available for displays and various installations; special exhibits will be tied in with notable patriotic anniversaries and annual observances. Staff members will, from time to time, give brief educational talks to groups of visitors in the auditorium. There will be a room devoted to nationality-music and folklore dramatizations, and the library will contain a special collection of material on the history of immigration and the contributions of immigrant groups.

A new, illustrated 48-page pamphlet, *In Quest of Freedom,* has been published by the United States Information Agency, Washington, D.C., describing the contributions made to America by immigrants and outstanding patriots of other lands who had sought refuge on our shores. In the last ten years the United States has accepted two million new permanent residents from abroad.

There is room in this great and good American family for all the diversities the Creator has produced in man. Our Constitution and Bill of Rights were, indeed, written to accommodate each and every minority, regardless of color, nationality, or creed. That is our democratic faith. Out of that diversity can come a unity the world has never witnessed. The need these days is to practice and preach that democratic faith. But we must first redeem it. The history of man's struggle to be free is in large degree a struggle to be free of oppressive procedures; the right to be free from torture and the hated oaths; the right to trial by jury; the right to confront the accuser face to face; the right to know the charge and to have a fair opportunity to defend; the right to speak and to write freely; the right to worship God as one chooses; the sanctity of the conscience; the right to be let alone; the dependency of the Government on the "consent of the governed."

JUSTICE WM. O. DOUGLAS, *An Almanac of Liberty;* Doubleday & Co., 1954.

The people of no other nation on earth enjoy the in-

herited advantages possessed by Americans to make
world-wide contacts between foreigners and themselves.
We are a people born of many peoples. Our country de-
veloped and grew through the combined efforts of all of
the people of the world. Our culture and our schools
have been shaped for three centuries by immigrants who
have come to our shores.

> EUGENE W. CASTLE, *The Great Giveaway: The*
> *Realities of Foreign Aid;* Henry Regnery Co., 1957.

The present is our indubitable own; we can shape it, for
we can shape ourselves; we can shape it as near to the
Heart's Desire as we have constancy and courage. We can
live without dishonor, and to live without dishonor is
to live with a high heart, and in such fashion as we shall
not wince when we look back upon our past. We are
indeed the masters of our fate—and, if only we shall
prove steadfast and unperturbed, above the "globes
clustered like evil eggs," we too shall see the stars.

> JUDGE LEARNED HAND, *The Spirit of Liberty;*
> Alfred A. Knopf, 1952.

IN NEW ENGLAND—I

History is not merely a great teacher of patriotism, but the one indispensable teacher; the more we know about the struggles which made the nation, the great men who led it, and the principles which sustained its people in time of trial, the deeper will be our feeling for our country. . . .

Simultaneously, our ideas of democracy have been enlarged. We used to say that the United States was unique in giving free self-government its largest and fullest test; that what Britain, Holland, and Switzerland did on a limited scale we did with tremendous sweep and amplitude. That was true. But political democracy is not enough. Social democracy, the abolition of race lines, class lines, and educational lines, is quite as important. So is economic democracy, the erasing of the old lines between rich and poor, the enactment of laws to make vast fortunes impossible, and the establishment of a welfare system which gives security to all.

And finally, the immense changes wrought by science and technology have given us a vision both of terrible new perils, and of dazzling vistas of comfort, happiness,

and moral and intellectual growth. The wonders of mass
production, of applied chemistry and physics, and of the
tapping of nuclear energy have created for us a new
world: a world in which America finds the problem of
peace desperately urgent, but also faces the possibilities
of a brighter era than was within the conception of our
ancestors.

ALLAN NEVINS, introduction to *The American Story*,
edited by Earl Schenck Miers; Channel Press, 1956.

America likes to keep memories green—memories of
courage, mostly; of accomplishment; of vision; of faith.
What else is the past but the inspiration for the future?
The cynic may belittle our bygone glories; but the cynic
never pretends to be a savior; his is the role of the defamer.
The swath of civilization rips its way across the towns and
the cities and the countryside to make new traffic arteries,
but the sacred places are generally spared.

Up and down New England—the haunts of patriots and
poets and pundits; of orators, educators and high-church
men; of village greens and commons and ancient seaports;
of graceful architecture and symphonies—countless historic
landmarks have been preserved for our edification. In Boston
—the Hub of the Revolution if not, as some legend-makers
would have it, "the Hub of the Universe"—Faneuil Hall,
the Cradle of Liberty, once echoed with the protests of
Samuel Adams, Daniel Webster, Wendell Phillips, and others
against the encroachments of the Crown. Given to the city
by Peter Faneuil, a Boston merchant, the two-story building
is a town hall above, public market below. Its noted steeple
adornment is a grasshopper weather vane, modeled by Shem
Drowne, of Hawthorne's story, the device having been chosen
because, while chasing one as a small boy, Drowne had met
the man who started him on the road to success. From the
belfry of Old North Church the lantern signals were flashed
to the silversmith-patriot Paul Revere, giving word of the
approach of the British: "One if by land; two if by sea."

The Old State House saw the Boston massacre take place beneath the stately carvings of the lion and the unicorn which adorn its roof. Lexington and Concord saw the British Redcoats under Gen. Gage routed in the first battles of the war in April, 1775; and the statue of the Minuteman is inscribed with Emerson's well-remembered lines:

> By the rude bridge that arched the flood,
> Their flag to April's breeze unfurled.
> Here, once the embattled farmers stood,
> And fired the shot heard round the world.

Salem has survived the vicissitudes of economic fortunes and is one of New England's treasurehouses, with its museum and quaint and graceful homes. Not a deep-water port, its flourishing foreign trade collapsed with the advent of deep-draft vessels. The frigate *Constitution*—"Old Ironsides"—rides at anchor in Salem Harbor. Nantucket, thirty miles out to sea, with its cobblestone streets and widows' walks, is one of America's few island shrines. An historic base for whalers, the Whaling Museum is full of the lore of these hardy adventurers.

Some thirty buildings, gathered from all over New England, were brought to Sturbridge—Old Sturbridge—to form a typical Yankee township of 1790, a teeming community affording an intimate glimpse of America in its early manhood. Grouped around the village green, the post-Revolutionary buildings contains a tavern, a general store, a schoolhouse, a sawmill, a gristmill, a smithy, shops and dwellings, with the meeting house—formerly the Fiskdale Baptist Church, taken from Middlesex—as the focal point. The village is a nonprofit educational institution that attracts tens of thousands of visitors during its seven-month season. On Lafayette Day a costumed pageant is held, with the French ally riding into town in the same coach in which he rode with Daniel Webster during his visit to America, for the laying of the cornerstone of Bunker Hill Monument on

Breed's Hill, in Charlestown, in 1825. At the base of the monument, a statue has been erected of Col. William Prescott, who gave the memorable command to his troops: "Don't fire until you see the whites of their eyes." Across the Massachusetts line in New Hampshire, near the township of Franklin is the memorial to the renowned orator, statesman and eloquent advocate, Daniel Webster. The shrine is a replica of Webster's birthplace and farm and contains numerous mementos of his life.

> Whether we look to the first charter of Virginia, or to that of Massachusetts Bay, or to the fundamental Orders of Connecticut, the same objective is present—a Christian land governed by Christian people, to whom no great harm can come, whose blessings of freedom of belief, of expression, of assembly, of petition, the sanctity of the home, equal justice under law, and the reservation of powers to the people, stem from the Christian religion.
>
> CHIEF JUSTICE EARL WARREN

> In America, it is evident that democracy is legitimate, that it springs from an undefiled source. America is completely the contrary of the nation of prey: she is wretched over the necessity for making herself feared, and she cannot bear to be hated. Her great errors have always been in the realm of the emotions. This nation is Christian and it is pious. The great Annunciation of this modern world, that "God is dead," missed America.
>
> REV. R. L. BRUCKBERGER, *One Sky to Share;* P. J. Kenedy & Sons, 1952.

IN NEW ENGLAND—II

And on the barren rock of Plymouth they kindled the
first pale beacon-fire of liberty—a fire whose spreading
flame burned up through a revolution that was destined
to change all the political theories and politics of ages
past; and which at this moment consumes not, but warms
into delightful and glorious existence the inhabitants of
an empire extending from the Atlantic to the Pacific;
from near the Tropic to the Arctic circle; and which
illuminates and cheers onward the whole civilized world!
There is no other world for another Columbus to discover, and unless the wheels of time can be stayed in
their tracks there can be no possible combination of circumstances, no possible series of events, that shall be so
favorable to the formation of a pure representative democracy, as those circumstances which were combined, and
those events which did transpire, to consummate the

51

establishment of our government. Freedom, driven from the old states, sought in this virgin world her last asylum, her noblest, fairest, final home.

From an oration delivered by George Holley on the Fourth of July, 1839, at Peru, Illinois.

We have come to cherish symbols of hardship and hardihood, man's struggle for progress and achievement, reminders of an enchanting past. For over the years many things have gone out of American life, things that stir happy recollections and bring back old associations—discarded insignia of American civilization. Life as our ancestors found it may seem to us limited and leisureless; doing everything oneself from dawn to dusk. But to them it was, nonetheless, a good life and doubtless they, too, found time for laughter, and song, and love, and piety, and hope.

When bent upon a nostalgic rendezvous, we turn our steps toward New England, with its wealth of shrines and restorations and well preserved antiquities.

Of all the categories of Americana, perhaps nothing imparts the flavor of "the good old days" so much as the open-air trolley, which took folks from sweltering Main Street to the refreshing countryside—all for a nickel, and no horn-tooting or traffic jams or flaring tempers.

The coastal village of Kennebunkport in Maine has become the end of the line for this fast-vanishing conveyance. There, a group of street-railway enthusiasts have set up an outdoor museum as a fitting resting place for the ancient tramcars in an area known as the Seashore Electric Railway, with a collection of some fifty open "twelve-benchers," and free rides around the half-mile track. The gentlemen in charge of these old sway-and-pitch juggernauts, with the burnt-out smell of electricity and the nervous throb of the air pump, were amiable custodians, the motorman taking no offense if you jostled him a bit as you sought a choice place right next to him, and the conductor calling out the stops as he made his way deftly along the running board, transfer stubs held tightly between his teeth. Later generations will never know what they missed!

And at Shelburne in Vermont is the Shelburne Museum, replete with buildings, furnishings, ornaments, and utilities assembled after years of search and research: the covered bridge; the 1830 schoolhouse, with drawings and scribblings on the walls just as the boys and girls of other days had left them; the country store, with its cracker barrel, soapstone stove, jiggle chair, post office, weather vanes, pewter tableware, quilts, and wooden Indians; the old red barn, the Stagecoach Inn, the Shaker Shed, the Cavendish Homestead. And here the side-wheel excursion steamer *Ticonderoga,* after forty-nine years of service on Lake Champlain, has been trundled two miles overland to come to rest, finally, beached on the museum's spacious front lawn:

Something of America steamed away,
On the cindery decks where the violins play:
Something of America followed the track
Of the paddlewheeled boat, and it never came back.
The paddlewheels stopped, and the walking beam;
Excursions ended in a land-locked dream
At a mooring upstream, far, far upstream,
Beyond the wharves of the morning.
                    ROBERT HILLYER, *The Suburb by the Sea;*
                    Alfred A. Knopf, 1952.

The guiding spirit of this distinctive enterprise, Mrs. J. Watson Webb, has been given an honorary degree of Master of Arts by Yale University, with the accompanying citation: "With discernment and affection you have assembled in your folk museum great collections of early American arts and crafts. There blacksmith, weaver, carpenter and painter ply again their felicitous trades. You have brought the American past into its own for the delight and edification of the present."

In Connecticut, a place of especial interest is Mystic,

where a whole New England seaport has come to life, with
rich memorabilia of vessels and of the sea and seafarers.
Craft of diverse kind that carried American colors and her
courage are preserved here, reminding us that ships discovered this country and have made possible its greatness.
From 1850 to 1870, this tiny port on the tidewaters of the
Mystic River became a major ship-building center, with
forty shipyards credited with nearly a thousand ships—ships
that went round Cape Horn or the Cape of Good Hope to
California, to China, and to India; ships that plied the whaling grounds of the world. In its heyday, Mystic produced
more famous captains, greater tonnage of fine ships, and a
larger number of distinguished sailing records than any
place of comparable size in the world. Present-day Mystic
is a reconstructed Yankee coastal village of the nineteenth
century, recreating one of the most dramatic and eventful
epochs of our country, when men of strength and courage
and self-reliance went down to the sea in the ships they had
made and set sail on perilous voyages to chart sea lanes
around the world.

A while ago, the son of one of Mystic's noted ship captains pieced together this fanciful word picture of the bustling harbor of long ago: "They came from all the oceans and
all the seas . . . out of the sea depths, out of the ice and
storm, out of oblivion. At dusk they came in from the sea
. . . moved up the river, one by one, silently on the floodtide
with the last breath of the evening wind . . . the whaleships
and the great clippers, the old-time packets, the fishing
smacks, the coasters, and the yachts. In the deepening gloom
they warped into their places side by side at the mouldering
wharves where long ago they had fitted out for sea. And the
shadow of the ships grew until it seemed to over-reach the
river. And then, from somewhere in the night, there came
a hail that the ships were all in."

And many of those stalwart mariners would doubtless
have concurred in this fine passage from W. MacNeile
Dixon's *The Human Situation* (Longmans, Green & Co.,

1950) : "Life is like the sea—untamed, moody, capricious, perilous. Men are said to love flattery. The sea never flatters. They are said to love ease. The sea offers toil. Like life, she deals in every form of danger. Like life, she strips men of their pretensions and their vanities, exposes the weakness of the weak and the folly of the fool. She flings a challenge— and human nature rises to a challenge."

At Hingham, Massachusetts, the Old Ship Meeting House, perhaps the oldest church building in continuous use in the United States, has observed its 275th anniversary. It is so named because the timbers supporting the roof give the effect of the inverted hull of a vessel under construction. The congregation follows the ancient custom of turning to face the choir loft in the rear of the church so that "all might sing together lustily" the closing hymn of Sunday service.

When I was a boy, my parents took me all over the country, pointing out the many historic places associated with great men and great events and explaining how the old scenes and means of livelihood helped one to recall how it was in those days. This looking back to our beginnings has spread throughout the land, the uncertainties and confusions of the present prompting us, perhaps, to search our past for the assurance of strength.

CORNELIUS VANDERBILT, JR.,
The Living Past of America; Crown, 1955.

The American is a new man who acts upon new principles—whose labours and posterity will one day cause great change in the world—they will finish the great circle. No part of his industry is claimed either by a despotic prince, a rich abbot, or a mighty lord; from involuntary idleness, servile dependence, penury and useless labor, he has passed to toils of a very different nature.

JEAN DE CREVECOEUR,
Letters From an American Farmer; 1782.

THE OLDEST LIVING THINGS

We enter the wood. The world that is so much with us is wholly gone. We tread the silent glades in silence. Here is the reign of peace. Beneath these shady boughs shall we not come to truth? Could we sit long enough in this untrespassed calm we would balk the screaming duties that are not real, and flaunt the clock that we call time. Then we, too, would be enlightened. Trees are friends to us, and in their presence, amidst the calm of their cathedral aisles, we meditate upon the blessedness of life.

JOHN STEWART COLLIS,
The Triumph of the Tree;
William Sloane Associates, 1954.

For quiet is not empty but full of meaning; silence helps one enter into more elevated spheres and listen to the mysterious voice of God.

POPE PIUS XII

More than fifty million persons are visiting our national

parks and other Federal recreation areas every year; in another decade, the annual trek will reach eighty million, and to accommodate this number adequately the National Park Service is faced with a ten-year improvement program costing some $786,000,000.

Pilgrims to the far country never fail to pause at Sequoia National Park, that land of enchantment and shrine of reflection. Named after a Cherokee Indian—Se-quo'-yah—this six-hundred-square-mile asylum on the western slopes of the Sierra crest in California takes in the 14,000-foot summit of Mount Whitney and is steeped in wild grandeur and breath-taking scenery. It was established in 1890 after many years of effort by public-spirited citizens intent upon preserving its groves of big trees from avaricious lumbermen.

Within this hallowed reservation stand the giant trees, making their ennobling contribution to the America we call "the Beautiful." From man's beginning, trees have been regarded with solemn awe, commanding an ancient reverence. In mythology, they were held in the esteem of the gods; groves were dedicated as temples; momentous pacts and solemn convocations have taken place where they threw their shadows. The oldest now-living things on earth, some of the sequoias that took root before the dawn of Christendom still beckon us to contemplate their splendor and to be grateful for their spiritual benefaction.

The largest specimen of the "big tree" is here—the General Sherman, towering 300 feet into the heavens. Reckoned to be more than three thousand years old, this patriarch weighs two thousand tons and has a circumference at its base of more than 100 feet. Under the vigilant protection of conservation authorities, the ax of the despoiler has been stayed and outrageous depredations halted, so that God's timeless treasury of trees might survive the centuries.

In the White Mountains of Inyo National Forest, the United State Forest Service recently located three California specimens—the bristlecone pine—whose life span has been scientifically established as approximately forty centuries.

Found on the forbidding peaks at timber line at an elevation of more than 10,000 feet, these scrubby hermits of the plant kingdom now join the ranks of earth's oldest known living things. Seldom noticed by people of the lowlands, these rare Methuselahs attain an average heights of less than 30 feet, each with a short, stocky trunk only two or three feet in diameter.

In every man's life pilgrimage, however unblessed, there are holy places where he is made to feel the kinship of the Divine; where the heavens bend low over his head and the angels come and minister unto him. These are the places of sacrifice, the meeting ground of mortal and immortal, the tents of trial wherein are waged the great spiritual combats of man's life.

MICHAEL MONAHAN, *Elbert Hubbard's Scrapbook;* Wm. H. Wise & Co., 1952.

Not in a hundred years would there be time to encompass all the glories of the American continent that is our birthright—timeless things, historic things, wondrous things, sacred things, and, above all, the endless enjoyment of the earth: "a minor ecstasy, a bit of star dust, which are for all of us, however monotonous our days and cramped our lives, however limited our opportunities; a fleeting instant when we lose ourselves in joy and wonder."

In the Black Hills of Wyoming stands our earliest National Monument—Devils Tower—the first such site to have been established under an Act of Congress, in 1906 following President Theodore Roosevelt's proclamation of Federal protection. This natural formation of uncertain origin is a mammoth column of solid rock with fluted sides and resembling a colossal petrified tree trunk. It is 1,000 feet in diameter at its base, rising 1,200 feet from the Belle Fourche River bed, and on a clear day can be seen for a hundred miles. Geologists reckon that it may date back over eons of time, perhaps fifty million years. It has been said that the Black Hills represent only a brief span between the past and the present—a single lifetime would bridge it: Custer to Coolidge; gold to uranium—the hills "will never grow old, because they have been young too long."

It is expected that more than two million sightseers will have visited Yellowstone National Park in 1956, and each year the influx to this most amazing of nature's "spectaculars" steadily increases, taxing the present facilities and calling for ever-amplified accommodations. And always a safari to this scenic cornucopia is well rewarded: a couple of hundred geysers in constant turmoil, headed by Old Faithful, which erupts unfailingly "every hour on the hour," tossing fountains of boiling water high into the air; waterfalls, sizzling pools, volcanoes, beautiful lakes, herds of wild animals roaming the dense, encircling forests. This fantastic fairyland comprises a reservation of some 2,000,000 acres, created by the Government in 1872, mostly in Wyoming, but spilling over into Montana and Idaho. The primitive Indians shunned it altogether, regarding it as an abode of evil spirits.

First to look upon the violent antics and mysteries of Yellowstone was John Colter, one of the lost men of American exploration. A member of the Lewis and Clark expedition, with its mandate from Thomas Jefferson to traverse and map the western country, Colter elected to set out alone in 1807 on a solitary journey through a perilous region which no white man had ever surveyed. After incredible escapes from the savage red men he came finally upon the gateway to the glories of the West which led to Yellowstone.

The spirit of a tree is our spirit. Every tree has little intimate signs that point the way to discoveries of the spirit, of art, of mechanics, of astonishment at natural miracles, and of reassurance about life itself in a violent world.

RUTHERFORD PLATT, *American Trees: A Book of Discovery;* Dodd, Mead & Co., 1952.

An infinite joy is lost to the world by the want of culture of this spiritual endowment. The greatest truths are wronged if not linked with beauty, and they win their way most surely and deeply into the soul when arrayed in this their natural and fit attire.

W. E. CHANNING (1780-1842)

THE CAROLINAS—I

Most Southerners know very well that the hallmark of America is freedom, that her symbols are the Liberty Bell and the Statue of Liberty, and that her machinery for maintaining freedom is not an end in itself but a means whereby each person should have the chance to develop all the excellence in him, that America is not free for nothing but for *something*.

WILLIAM T. POLK,
Southern Accent: From Uncle Remus to Oak Ridge;
William Morrow & Co., 1953.

Despairing patriots who insist upon mourning what they call the disappearance of the American frontier can leave off wringing of the hands and give thought to the South—the bustling, forward-looking, rejuvenated South, the Dixie with the new look. And they might retrieve their defection by saving their Confederate money—for the South is rising again! Below the Mason and Dixon Line is being unfolded a vast and varied domain abounding in historic, cultural, and recreational areas of such absorbing interest as to dwarf the old frontiers of the West, which are now mostly history or legend. And economically, the South has been transformed from one of the nation's gravest problems to the nation's greatest economic opportunity. Culturally, too, the South is "breaking out all over" with significant achievements to its credit in literature, drama, art, and music and with Pulitzer-prize winners and best-sellers adorning many of "the provinces."

"A striking feature of Southern life is that it is much more conversational than life in the North. The fact has a bearing on literature: if many Southerners write well, that is partly because Southerners as a type are good talkers. They become good talkers by practice and social custom, but also by necessity. Chiefly they talked about persons dead and living. They told stories about their own families and their own neighborhoods." (Malcolm Cowley, *Great Tales of The Deep South.*)

While not properly the gateway to the South, the Carolinas will admirably serve as an introduction to that gracious, if turbulent realm of ancient manors and manners, customs and traditions of an age of so-called chivalry.

Entering North Carolina from the Great Smoky National Reservation—half in that state and half in Tennessee —the visitor encounters a magnificent park of half a million acres, with sixteen mountain peaks topping 6,000 feet, a living museum where he may see how the mountain people live and how they work at their ancient crafts and hear their proud history recited in dramas staged among the valleys and the hills. Great Smoky is the most majestic of the state's eleven national parks and forests.

Descending to the sea coast, one finds a variety of historic places and pleasure grounds. Cape Hatteras National Seashore Recreation area is one of very few such public parks established along our ocean beaches, a coast line extending 3,700 miles from Maine to Texas; one of our unique national resources—a literally irreplaceable asset rich in bio-logical, historical, and recreational value. *Our Vanishing Shoreline,* prepared by the National Park Service, is re-garded as one of the important reports of our decade in the field of essential conservation.

Fort Raleigh on Roanoke Island is the site of the first English colony in America (1585) ; and here Virginia Dare was born, the first American child of English parentage. There is the furnished two-room shack at Raleigh where a tailor's apprentice, Andrew Johnson, was born—who, after moving with his family to Tennessee, was to become the nation's seventeenth President, following Lincoln's assassin-ation.

The Old Salem restoration, an eighteenth-century Mora-vian Church settlement now approaching its two-hundredth anniversary, is a charming oasis of history almost completely surrounded by the bustling tobacco center of Winston-Salem. The Wachovia Museum houses one of the most im-portant collections of local antiquities in the United States; and the village's tree-shaded graveyard—God's Acre—has been the scene of the Moravian Easter-sunrise service for more than one hundred years.

The tourist will be well repaid by putting on his itiner-ary the outdoor shrine at the hamlet of Fletcher in an evergreen enclosure at the Calvary Episcopal Church. A Confederate barracks during the Civil War, the site is a sentimental memorial commemorating a roster of southern immortals with monuments of rough-hewn native granite carrying a bronze plaque with appropriate quotations. Among the honored statesmen, poets, writers, musicians, and benefactors are Robert E. Lee, Jefferson Davis, Joel Chand-ler Harris, Francis Scott Key, John Fox, Jr., Stephen Collins Foster, O. Henry, James Whitcomb Riley . . .

And, of course, the Kill Devil Hill monument, com-memorating man's first flight in an engine-driven 'plane at Kitty Hawk in 1903 . . . The brothers Wright, makers of bicycles in Dayton, Ohio, had brought their fragile, 12-

horsepower frame to this lonely stretch of beach, and Orville, crawling to a prone position between the wings, had kept the biplane air-borne for 59 seconds over a stretch of 852 feet—man's first precarious invasion of the "untrespassed sanctity of space." Ever since man found out about the wheel, his consuming ambition has been to fly—his stubborn challenge from the beginning of recorded history. Even the mythology of the Greeks had its ill-starred Icarus—Icarus the venturesome—who fell a derelict into the open sea when the sun's too intemperate heat melted away his wings.

As we celebrate another anniversary of the epochal achievement of powered flight, we at once reflect upon "what a piece of work is man," that he should achieve in the brief hours of half a century such an incredible conquest, perhaps the final revolutionary function in human affairs.

And yet time—and talent—have a way of playing tricks on prophetic souls. There is the story of the bishop who many years ago professed his belief that all the prophecies had been fulfilled, all great inventions accomplished, the millennium was at hand, the day of judgment not far off. His host dissented, giving it as his opinion that there would be more startling inventions in the next fifty years than in all previous time; that man would even learn to fly like the birds—even faster than the birds! Whereupon the good bishop flew into a rage and exclaimed: "My dear sir, it is given only to God and the angels to fly."

The bishop was Bishop Wright, the father of Orville and Wilbur!

Whatever man imagines, he can obtain—if he doesn't become too arrogant and encroach upon the rights of the gods. Is aviation too arrogant? I don't know. Sometimes flying feels too godlike to be attained by man. Is man encroaching upon a forbidden realm? Is aviation dangerous because the sky was never meant for him? When one obtains too great a vision, is there some power that draws one from mortal life forever? Or do the gods retire as science and commerce advance?

CHARLES A. LINDBERGH,
The Spirit of St. Louis; Scribner's, 1953.

THE CAROLINAS—II

There is something about a river that speaks to the hearts of all men in a language each can understand, in a song of endless significance and beauty. It speaks to man of the days of the earth before his coming, of his slow beginnings and turbulent progress, of his eternal kinship with the spirit of the universe, of his ancient heritage and his infinite progress. As time moves on as inexorably as the waters follow their age-old course to the sea, the old Santee will yet witness here as varied scenes as those it remembers from time long past.

HENRY SAVAGE, JR.,
The Santee: River of the Carolinas;
Rinehart & Co., 1956.

The hundred and fifty miles of the Santee run across the state of South Carolina—"a fair and spacious province" —from the mountains to the sea, gathering up in its currents historic places and events both of the old South and of the new. The Spaniards, intent upon empire, came to its shores in 1526 but stayed only until fever and desertions and Indians snuffed out their dream; it witnessed the coming of Huguenot refugees from France and the birth of an aristocracy built upon the flimsy one-crop economy of cotton—and slavery. South Carolina was the first state to secede from the Union and the Santee saw the guns from Fort Moultrie silence the garrison on Fort Sumter—the "battle of the forts," the opening encounter in the Civil War. Today, after the demoralizing vicissitudes of plundering and reconstruction, the Santee rolls proudly through the thriving centers of diversified industry whose wheels its restless waters help to turn. When George III inquired of Lord Cornwallis whether or not he thought the province of South Carolina was worth conquering, the response came back: "Tell His Majesty, yes, if for no other reason than the succulent bream in the Santee."

The Palmetto State boasts an imposing roster of native-born patriots: Gen. William Moultrie, defender of Charleston; Francis Marion, "the swamp fox"; Andrew Jackson, seventh President of the United States; John Caldwell Calhoun, Vice-President, 1825-32, foremost champion of states' rights; Wade Hampton, general, governor, and senator; Charles Cotesworth Pinckney, signer of the Constitution; Thomas Heyward, signer of the Declaration—as well as a coterie of distinguished writers, painters, musicians, and architects.

Charleston, or Charles Town, as it was originally called when settled in 1670 by the English, is the enduring shrine that sets South Carolina apart from her sister states, for here one finds the uncontaminated air and grace of the old South. The people of Charleston love the South and love their city best of all. Their ancestors fought hard to preserve it, and the citizens who have followed them like to bask in its distinctive culture and pervading charm. The original Charlestonians were obliged to stand off inroads by the Spanish, the French, the British; the depredations of the Union

forces; the violent antics of nature. Meticulous restorations
have brought back most of the beauties and flavor of its past.
Its highways and byways, its urban and rural rallying places,
its first families and latter day sons carry names to conjure
with. Located at the juncture of two large rivers, some wag
about town long ago insisted that "the Ashley and the Cooper
came together to form the Atlantic Ocean."

And in his pictorial album *The Living Past of America,*
Cornelius Vanderbilt, Jr., spells out the charm of the city:
"We have only a few cities left with a real flavor of their
own—Boston, Washington, New Orleans, St. Augustine, San
Francisco, San Diego. But we have only one Charleston, and
it is to the people, with their love of the gracious way in
which our ancestors lived, that we owe a real debt of gratitude for keeping Old Charleston old. It is the only historical
city in America today in which people still live as they
used to live, where life continues much as it was in the time
of our forefathers—the exquisite old houses, lovely furnishings, interesting people, and a penchant for keeping history
historical in the niche it should always be."

And the late Ludwig Lewisohn observed: "A race lived
here that loved dignity without ostentation, books and wine
and human distinction. Its sins, which were many, fade into
the past. They were always less vulgar and ugly than the
sins of those who have come after."

Clustered around this citadel of charm and splendor are
any number of lesser but hardly less-interesting places of
historic interest: the Dock Street Theatre, at Church and
Queen streets, one of the earliest playhouses in America;
the Miles Brewton House, headquarters for Sir Henry Clinton and other British commanders during the Revolution;
the impressive statue of Pitt the Elder, erected by the colonists for his intervention in behalf of American liberty. Speaking in the House of Commons, Pitt had exclaimed, "They
tell us that America is obstinate, that America is almost in
open rebellion. I rejoice that America has resisted! Three
millions of people so dead to all the feelings of liberty as

voluntarily to submit to be slaves would have been fit instruments to make slaves of all the rest; necessity is the plea for every infringement of human freedom. It is the argument of tyrants." And further, the Heyward House, where Washington was entertained in 1791; the slave market; the powder magazine; the Battery; the old Capitol; the City Hall; the Sword Gates, a wrought-iron masterpiece in a city of famous gateways; and a score of museums full of cherished antiquities.

In the adjoining graveyard of St. Michael's Episcopal Church, one comes upon the oft-quoted epitaph of James Louis Petigru, the leading Unionist of South Carolina:

Unawed by Opinion,
Unseduced by Flattery:
Undismayed by Disaster,
He confronted life with antique Courage,
And Death with Christian Hope.
In the great Civil War
He withstood His People for his Country
But his People did homage to the man,
Who held his Conscience higher than their Praise;
    And his Country
Heaped her Honours upon the Grave of the Patriot,
    To whom, living,
His own righteous Self-Respect sufficed
Alike for Motive and Reward.

And the visitor may pause at another inscription—at the Monument to the Confederate Dead—this a stirring summary of southern ideals:

Let the Stranger,
Who may in Future Times
Read This Inscription,
Recognize That These Were Men
Whom Power Could Not Corrupt,

Whom Death Could Not Terrify,
Whom Defeat Could Not Dishonor,
And Let Their Virtues Plead
    For Just Judgment
Of the Cause in which They Perished.
Let the South Carolinians
Of another Generation Remember
That the State Taught Them
How to Live and How to Die.
And that from Her Broken Fortunes
She Has Preserved for Her Children
The Priceless Treasure of Their Memories,
Teaching All who may Claim
The Same Birthright
That Truth, Courage, and Patriotism
Endure Forever.

But the fairest heritage of all handed down by South
Carolinians are the Charleston gardens—Middleton, Magnolia, Runnymede, Cypress, Belle Isle—hallowed places, indeed, man's and nature's most prolific handiwork. Here is
an unsurpassed profusion of fragrance and color, a consummate skill of artistry and design, born of wealth and culture
and leisure—"a poetic kind of immortality." John Gals-
worthy, English playwright and poet, called the Magnolia
Gardens "the most beautiful spot in the world."—

Nothing so free and so gracious, so lovely and wistful;
nothing so richly colored yet so ghostlike, exists, planted
by the sons of men, a kind of paradise which has wandered down, a miraculously enchanted wilderness—

an inspiring addition to the author's varied catalogue of
beauty:

A choirboy's voice, a ship in sail, an opening flower, a
town at night, the song of the blackbird, a lovely poem,

leaf shadows, a child's grace, the starry skies, a cathedral, apple trees in spring, a thoroughbred horse, sheep-bells on a hill, a rippling stream, a butterfly, the crescent moon—the thousand sights or sounds or words that evoke in us the thought of beauty—these are the drops of rain that keep the human spirit from death by drought.

IN THE DEEPER SOUTH

Diversity in union and a regionalism that no longer
transcends nationalism are among the exhaustless de-
lights of America. If surveys of the folklore of New England and of the Old South differed from similar books
about other parts of the United States, for example, some
of the distinctive qualities that have shaped folklore have
been the British stock, the presence of the Negro almost
everywhere, the persistence of the Confederate tradition,
the dominance of staple agriculture, and a climate that
supplies outdoor themes for stories more appropriately
told under a shade tree than from a chimney corner. . . .
Behind the songs and stories often were inextinguish-
able humor, zeal, faith and acceptation, in a spirit almost
Hellenic, of the adversity man could not escape—a state
of mind the South needed when her cities were ashes and
her sons were slain. There is some dark laughter in South-

ern folklore; there is superstition, too; but there is manhood and mirth and cheer for dark nights.

DOUGLAS SOUTHALL FREEMAN in a foreword to
Southern Folklore, by B. A. Botkin; Crown, 1949.

Inherent in the glory that was the traditional South were
qualities often estimated to be the most distinctive and
glamorous in the American picture: . . . a certain heritage
abounding in the concepts and experience of good living,
strong loyalties, spiritual energy, personal distinctions,
and strong individuality. . . .

HOWARD W. ODUM; *ibid.*

Americans everywhere are indebted to the Garden Clubs
of Natchez—the Pilgrimage City—for sponsoring annual
tours through this enchanting section of the Mississippi
Southland, and for the untiring efforts of their members in
perpetuating the much-loved glories of the deep and gracious South of ante-bellum days. These fertile and fragrant
acres have witnessed Indian, French, Spanish, Union, and
Confederate designs upon them, all coveting, at one time
or another, a land rich in productivity and promise. From
the eighteenth-century buildings of early settlers to the ele-
gant mansions of the prosperous cotton-planters before the
blight of the Civil War, one may follow the growth of a
civilization which began from the wilderness. In the many
famous, time-mellowed homes—Arlington, Elgin Plantation,
Dunleith, The Elms, The Burn, Hope Farm, Holly Hedges,
D'Evereux, Stanton Hall—with their treasures of a vanished
era, there is enshrined the authentic history of the Natchez
country, recalling the days when the old capital was a queen
city of the lower Mississippi. It was named for the Natchez
Indians, and when founded by the French in 1716 was called
Fort Rosalie. The old tavern still stands at the end of the
long and treacherous Natchez Trace, a rough trail running
through the forests from Natchez to Nashville.

North from Natchez lies Vicksburg—"the Gibraltar of

the Confederacy"—finally reduced by Gen. Grant after a siege of almost three months while the Confederate garrison waited for relief from Johnston's army, which never came. With the fall of Vicksburg the southern cause was doomed. The National Military Park contains 230 monuments, 900 historical tablets, and statues of the victorious Union general and of the gallant defender, Gen. Pemberton. Downtown Vicksburg museums depict life on the old Mississippi, and the city houses one of the largest collections of Confederate relics in the South.

Down on the Gulf Coast, Biloxi is the oldest French city in the United States, settled in 1699 by Pierre Lemoyne d'Iberville, and has come to be known as "the shrine of the shrimp." A colorful ceremony of nation-wide interest is the annual blessing of the shrimp fleet, a custom going back to the shores of the Adriatic and to the Normandy coast. The pageant is presided over by Catholic priests to invoke the Lord's blessing, a peaceful voyage, an abundant catch, and a safe harbor.

In the Bayou Land of Louisiana there is the Shrine of Merriment—the fabulous Mardi Gras revels at New Orleans, a fortnight of sumptuous balls, masques, dancing, and floats culminating on Shrove Tuesday. The city itself has a backdrop of Old World flavor in a modern metropolis. Founded by the French in 1718 and named after the Duke of Orléans, the place has never relinquished its foreign air—its buildings replete with balconies, balustrades, intricate ironwork, its patios with exotic planting, its quaint byways and alleys; St. Louis Cathedral in Jackson Square, the latter named after the hero of the battle of New Orleans, is one of the most revered churches in America; the Absinthe House in Bourbon Street was the favorite rendezvous of Jean Pierre Lafitte, the crafty pirate; the Cabildo, completed in 1799, served as the City Hall for many years and here the Louisiana Purchase effected by Thomas Jefferson was formally ratified, France ceding to the United States for the trifling sum of fifteen million dollars a vast domain of five hundred million acres stretching all the way to the Rocky Mountains and the present Canadian border.

Scattered up and down the Florida peninsula are many places of antiquity which still embellish the American scene. The modern story of North America began in 1513 when the Spaniard Ponce de León, seeking the legendary "fountain of youth," went ashore on a land he called *La Florida,* where he pressed his fruitless search. In 1565 another Spaniard, Admiral Menendez de Avilés, founded the first permanent white settlement in America—St. Augustine—far up on the east coast around which cluster some of the oldest historical associations of any of our cities. This first American shrine is approaching its four-hundredth anniversary. Established fifty-five years before the Pilgrims came, St. Augustine looks back over a longer span of Western civilization than any other city in the land. The market place and public auction square, the ramparts of the fortress Castillo de San Marcos, the Lightner Museum, its gates and walls and "narrow gauge" thoroughfares, the unusual detail of its architecture, entitle it to rank as America's heirloom. At De Funiak Springs, on the lawn of the Walton County Courthouse on the Old Spanish Trail, was erected, in 1871, the first monument to Confederate soldiers in the South.

And the St. Johns River, rising in Lake Washington in the saw-grass country and emptying into the Atlantic, is one of the few rivers in the world flowing north, and it has probably seen as much history as any river in America. In the little town of White Springs on the banks of the now-famous Suwannee River a memorial has been completed honoring Stephen Foster, who wrote "Old Folks at Home" —which has been adopted by Florida as its state song—and many other immortal melodies. Further south, some thirty miles from Miami, one encounters a sanctuary perhaps twice as old as St. Augustine—the ancient Spanish Monastery of St. Bernard of Sacramenia, whose 36,000 stones were crated and shipped and reassembled on its present New World site. The Ringling Museum of Art at Sarasota contains many of the canvases of Rubens, Rembrandt, Frans Hals, El Greco, Velázquez, Sir Joshua Reynolds, and Gainsborough.

The enlightened economic revolution going on in the South is graphically portrayed in a speech delivered some sixty years ago by one Henry W. Grady, of Georgia, in which he describes the funeral arrangements for an old crony: "They cut through solid marble to make his grave, and yet the tombstone they put above him came from Vermont; they buried him in a pine forest, and yet his pine coffin was made in Cincinnati; he lies within a stone's throw of an iron mine, and yet the nails in his coffin and the iron in the shovel that dug his grave were imported from Pittsburgh. They dressed him in a New York coat and a Boston pair of shoes, a pair of breeches made in Chicago and a shirt from Troy. The South didn't furnish a thing on earth for that funeral except the corpse and the hole in the ground."

Today, the Georgian's family could have buried him in acceptable style with all the requisites furnished by the land of Dixie without recourse to Yankee products.

We of the South stand in the midst of vast undeveloped resources. Here we have the climate, the sunshine, the rainfall, the soil and the people, the bountiful blessings of Almighty God, and, for the first time in our history, a substantial amount of liquid wealth, all beckoning us to a future unlimited for ourselves and for the generations that come after us.

A Former President of the American Bankers Association

I can conceive of nothing more foolish than to say the world is finished. We are not at the end of our progress, but at the beginning. We have but reached the shores of a great unexplored continent. We cannot turn back. . . . It is man's destiny to ponder the riddle of existence and, as a by-product of his wonderment, to create a new life on this earth.

CHARLES F. KETTERING

VALLEY FORGE

This government, the offspring of our own choice un-
influenced and unawed, adopted upon full investigation
and mature deliberation, completely free in its principles, in the distribution of its powers, uniting security
with energy, and containing within itself a provision for
its own amendment, has a just claim to your confidence
and your support. Respect for its authority, compliance
with its laws, acquiescence in its measures, are duties
enjoined by the fundamental maxims of true liberty.
The Constitution, until changed by an explicit and
authentic act of the whole people, is sacredly obligatory
upon all. The very idea of the power and the right of
the people to establish government presupposes the duty
of every individual to obey the established government.

Washington's Farewell Address

Valley Forge Park in Pennsylvania, the scene of Gen.
Washington's bleak and heartbreaking bivouac in the winter

of 1777–78, is one of America's most hallowed shrines, symbolizing as it does our dependence upon Divine Providence, if man is to triumph over adversity.

It was here that the leader of the Continental Army knelt in supplication with his tattered patriots that their cause—the cause of freedom from tyranny—might survive. Young in years, as time goes, its resolute spirit stemming from these birth throes when its life hung in the balance, the Republic did indeed survive, to be the rallying place, even, of the free nations of the whole world. It was at Valley Forge that the first great crisis in American history was resolved. More than a million visitors are attracted every year to the beauty and dignity of this place of meditation, the environs of which encompass the most sacred of American principles and traditions, inspiring a rededication to the priceless American heritage. Here we may keep bright our beginnings, be inspired by past achievements, and be made more aware of our duty.

"It may be doubted," in the opinion of Sir George Trevelyan, eminent English historian and military analyst, "whether so small a number of men ever employed so short a space of time with greater and more lasting results upon the history of the world."

The two thousand acres of the park include most of the historic site, which has been restored as nearly as possible to its original condition as a military camp: the redoubts, the soldiers' huts, the field hospitals, Washington's headquarters, and now the National Memorial Arch. The George Washington Memorial Chapel—the shrine of the American people—is dedicated to the glory of God and the memory of George Washington and his heroic band of volunteers. The Valley Forge Historic Society conducts the adjoining museum, and here faith and patriotism are kept constantly before the people, unsullied with sinister shadows, keeping alive forever in the memory of a grateful America as an immortal example of the high resolve which won their independence.

"What is the soul of a nation: It must be born, like all
else that is human, from suffering; the lives of many men,
through long years of history, must give it fragrance. It must
draw its strength from a great faith in something, Divine or
human. At some time in its history, the nation must have
read its fate in that invisible writing which becomes legible
only in the fierce light of a great peril."

Valley Forge is headquarters, also, of Freedoms Foundation, a nonprofit organization established in 1949 by a group
of public-spirited citizens intent upon promoting throughout the land the tried-and-true principles of Americanism so
that these may not be permitted to go unheeded in the unturned pages of American history. Each year, on Washington's Birthday, awards aggregating a hundred thousand dollars, together with the George Washington medals, are given
for outstanding achievements in bringing about a better
understanding of the American way of life. Recipients are
chosen from participants in a wide list of categories: writers
of editorials, community programs, school and college essays, company publications, letters from Armed Forces per-
sonnel, magazine articles; producers of 16-millimeter motion-picture films, radio programs, photographs; deliverers
of addresses and sermons.

"Our nation is not merely freedom of opportunity, or of
worship, or of assembly, or of the press. America represents
the spiritual and moral strength of a free people. It is the
composite of all that has been achieved to elevate our understanding and enable us to pursue our daily tasks, guided by
a standard of ethical principles that free men have come to
recognize as indispensable to their survival and the preservation of their liberties. America is truth and hope and faith
and courage and patience—the merits of which were born
long ago on these surrounding fields." (Clifford F. Hood,
at Valley Forge, February 22, 1955.)

Visitors will pause also at the near-by national shrine of
Washington's Crossing, Pennsylvania, whence the General
convoyed a force of 2,400 men across the ice-choked Dela-

ware in a surprise attack on the Hessian mercenaries at
Trenton on Christmas night, 1776, putting the garrison to
headlong rout. And a few miles from Gen. Washington's
headquarters is the first American home of John James
Audubon, the great naturalist-painter who devoted so many
years to the study of the rich bird life that still abounds in
the Valley of the Perkiomen. The dwelling houses a notable
collection of original folios that have brought him, for his
paintings, world-wide renown as the recognized biographer
of the feathered creatures of the kingdom of the air, in his
Birds of America. On display in the restoration is also one
of the world's most familiar paintings—Emanuel Leutze's
"Washington Crossing the Delaware."

Against the insidious wiles of foreign influence, I conjure you to believe me, fellow citizens, the jealousy of a
free people ought to be constantly awake, since history
and experience prove that foreign influence is one of the
most baneful foes of Republican government. So far as
we have already formed engagements with foreign countries, let them be fulfilled with perfect good faith. Here
let us stop. It should be our true policy to steer clear of
permanent alliances with any portion of the foreign
world. Why, indeed, quit our own to stand upon foreign
ground? Why, by interweaving our destiny with any part
of Europe, entangle our peace and prosperity in the toils
of European ambition, rivalship, interest, humor, or
caprice?

Washington's Farewell Address

THE PLACE OF HONOR

Washington, the brave, the wise, the good, supreme in war, in council, and in peace. Valiant without ambition, discreet without fear, confident without presumption.

In disaster, calm; in success, moderate; in all, himself.

The hero, the patriot, the Christian.

The father of nations, the friend of mankind, who, when he had won all, renounced all, and sought, in the bosom of his family and of nature, retirement, and in the hope of religion, immortality.

Inscription at Mount Vernon

The most hallowed shrine of all the Presidents, Mount Vernon stands on a high bluff looking out upon a broad curve of the Potomac, sixteen miles south of the city of Washington. Attracted by its graceful lines, the well-preserved buildings of the compound, and the countless mementos of the nation's beginnings, the visitor is inspired by the form and flavor of America's yesterdays as he reflects upon the notable achievements of the Great Man who still holds the first place of honor in the esteem of his country-

men. The estate is part of a large tract of land in northern
Virginia originally in a royal grant made to Lord Culpepper,
later becoming the property of Augustine, the father of
George, Washington, who changed the name of the planta-
tion from Hunting Creek to Mount Vernon in honor of
Admiral Vernon, under whom he had served in the West
Indies.

Inheriting the property in 1752, Washington, one of the
wealthiest men of his time in America, embellished and enlarged the homestead and set about making his inheritance
a self-contained farming unit of some 250 acres. Here he
brought his wife, Martha Dandridge Custis, but their residence was subject to protracted interruptions. During the
Revolution, Washington visited Mount Vernon only twice,
on the way to and from Yorktown in 1781, not to return
until two years later—leaving shortly thereafter again, to
become President, residing in New York and Philadelphia,
with only brief visits to the plantation.

Despite his multitudinous affairs of state, it was Washington's ambition to become the leading agriculturist in
America. He kept elaborate notes, corresponded about his
experiments with his neighbors, operated a dairy, smoke-
house, distillery, and gristmill, shipped his produce to market ports in his own schooner. He was deeply honored upon
receiving a sword from Frederick the Great and the keys to
the Bastille from Lafayette; but he took just as much pride
when the Agricultural Society awarded him a prize for
"raising the largest mule in the country."

Following the death of Washington, the "realm" was
offered for sale, but through the efforts of Miss Ann Pamela
Cunningham of South Carolina, by whom it was purchased
for two hundred thousand dollars in the name of the Mount
Vernon Ladies Association of the Union, it was saved for the
nation and posterity. The original furniture was reassembled; the buildings and garden restored to their early dignity. It is believed that sixteen trees planted by Washington
still flourish there, and the mammoth boxwood dates from

1798. A burial vault of plain brick overgrown with ivy holds the remains of Washington and those of his wife.

"On the 12th of December, 1799," writes Howard Swiggett in *The Great Man* (Doubleday, 1953), "he meticulously wrote out instructions for the rotation of crops, dictated a letter to Hamilton about a military academy at West Point, set down the prevailing weather conditions: on the morning of the 13th it was snowing, with the mercury down to 28 degrees. He called for his horse. Before the next day was done he died as a country gentleman should, after a snowy ride across his fields in that last winter twilight. The story of this wonderful life is one of stupendous success. Hardly a thing he strove for failed of achievement. Yet all his great deeds were done with modesty. Let his country have peace and independence and he would not have ventured twenty miles from Mount Vernon again."

While the idea of a memorial to Washington had been talked of ever since the close of the Revolutionary War, it was not until fifty years after his death that the cornerstone of the monument was laid and, because of numerous delays in construction, was not formally dedicated until 1885. Sharing place with the Lincoln and Jefferson memorial shrines in the Tidal Basin of the Potomac at Washington, D. C., the imposing white marble obelisk rises to a height of 555 feet, topped by a pyramid of solid aluminum. Set into the interior walls are 189 commemorative stones, bearing appropriate inscriptions, contributed by the forty-eight states and a number of foreign countries. A million persons every year view the giant shaft, and as many as fifteen thousand visitors in a single day have climbed its 898 steps or taken the slow-going lift to the summit.

His [Washington's] integrity was most pure, his justice the most inflexible I have ever known, no motives of interest or consanguinity, of friendship or hatred, being able to bias his decision. He was, indeed, in every sense of the word, a wise, a good, and a great man. On the whole, his character was, in its mass, perfect, in nothing bad, in few points, indifferent; and it may be truly said that never did nature and fortune combine more perfectly to make a man great and to place him in an everlasting remembrance.

THOMAS JEFFERSON

The Virginia dynasty devoted their lives to the new democracy that was to deny and then physically destroy the world of the landed aristocrat.

CLIFFORD DOWDEY,
The Great Plantation; Rinehart, 1957.

"THE LITTLE MOUNTAIN"

On the summit of one of the mountains we discovered
the house of Mr. Jefferson which stands pre-eminent in
its retirement. It was himself who built it, preferring this
vista among all others. It was a debt Nature owed to the
philosopher and a man of taste that in his own possession he should find a spot where he might best study
and enjoy Her. He called his home Monticello, being
the Italian for Little Mountain.

The Marquis de Chastellux (1734-1788)

This cherished hilltop dwelling place of a "many-sided
master of infinite subjects," whom history ranks as one of
the four immortals among the founders of the Republic,
has stood high in the affectionate attachment of the American people ever since it was retrieved from neglect and im-
pending ruin a hundred and fifty years ago and restored by
patriotic and public-spirited citizens.

A shrine of surpassing beauty overlooking the Blue

Ridge Mountains of Piedmont Virginia, Thomas Jefferson's Monticello, in Albemarle County, was twenty-five years in the building. He had a passionate love of architecture, and its design, construction, and landscaping were of his own conception and largely his own handiwork. With his broad enthusiasms, Jefferson—an early votary of the "do-it-yourself" cult—was constantly improving and improvising, lavishing money on tools and shops, new scientific and agricultural instruments, industrial machinery and novel inventions. Built in the Doric style, Monticello became under Jefferson's hand a place of rare artistry, with its heavy cornices and balustrades, doors of solid mahogany, and its many ingenious devices for comfort and utility.

During his tenure of the manor house—when not called away in the public service—he entertained extensively the gentry of renown; and it was to these gracious precincts that he brought his bride, Martha Wayles Skelton, a young widow. After his death in 1826 at the age of eighty-three, the estate, called Shadwell, was sold for debts and was later used as a hospital in the Civil War.

After a series of political vicissitudes—he was Secretary of State under Washington and later Vice-President—Thomas Jefferson served two terms, 1801–9, as third President of the United States, the first to be inaugurated in the city of Washington. An intellectual to his fingertips—the son of Peter Jefferson, Virginia planter, whose family traced back far in England and Scotland—he nevertheless eschewed snobbery and favored a broad diffusion of wealth. He was educated at William and Mary College in Williamsburg; his life was lived in a rich diversity of enterprise and accomplishment, rewarding to his country and his countrymen, dedicated to the image of moral freedom:

"I have sworn upon the altar of God," he wrote, "eternal hostility against every form of tyranny over the mind of man. Intellectual freedom is based on the illimitable freedom of the human mind. We must not be afraid to follow truth wherever it may lead, nor to tolerate any error so long as reason is left free to combat it."

Regarded as the founder of the present Democratic Party, Jefferson's masterpiece, of course, was his composing the Declaration of Independence. In the reforms he had wrought in Virginia he laid the cornerstone of that religious tolerance which was to become one of the most civilized contributions of the new nation to humanity. He stood with common sense and moderation for the ultimate elimination of slavery. As Minister to France, he achieved a brilliant success in establishing our international policy, saving the credit and honor of his country. He contributed notably in effecting the inclusion of the Bill of Rights in the Constitution. He raised the money, designed the buildings, with their arcades, pavilions and rotunda, well-planned lawns and ranges, of the University of Virginia at near-by Charlottesville—perhaps his fondest dream, and a thing of enduring beauty. He envisioned the westward sweep of the country to the Pacific Ocean; the Lewis and Clark Expedition, undertaken at his instance, opened up a vast new frontier. Under his regime he concluded the purchase from Napoleon of the Louisiana Territory, which, with its million square miles, doubled the area of the nation and has been called "the greatest real estate bargain in history." John Bakeless, in *The American Story*, calls the transaction "the making of the modern United States. It made possible the destiny of America as a two-ocean world power. It gave us control of some of the most fertile territory and some of the richest mines in the world; it gave us control of the Mississippi River, a vital commercial route; it united our country as nothing else could have done."

Descending the Mississippi River to the Gulf of Mexico, Robert Cavelier de La Salle, pioneer French explorer and settler, claimed the whole boundless valley for his King and named it Louisiana, only to be murdered by his own men in 1687. "Serious in all things, incapable of the lighter pleasures, incapable of repose, finding no joy but in the pursuit of great designs, too shy for society and too re-served for popularity, often unsympathetic and always seem-ing so, smothering emotions which he could not utter, schooled to universal distrust, stern to his followers and pitiless to himself, bearing the brunt of every hardship and every danger, demanding of others an equal constancy joined to an implicit deference, heeding no counsel but his own, attempting the impossible and grasping at what was too vast to hold—he contained in his own complex and pain-ful nature the chief springs of his triumphs, his failures and his death." (Francis Parkman, *The Discovery of The Great West: La Salle;* Rinehart, 1956.)

Jefferson had asked that this inscription be engraved on the headstone of his burial place, "and not one word more": "Here was buried Thomas Jefferson—author of the Declaration of Independence, of the Statute of Virginia for Religious Freedom, Father of the University of Virginia—because of these I wish to be remembered."

The Thomas Jefferson Memorial, one of the most im-pressive buildings in the capital, stands on the southern shore of the tidal basin in West Potomac Park. Its Pantheon style and simplicity of design represents Jefferson's artistic preference. The structure, done in marble, contains a cir-cular chamber with a domed ceiling, dominated by a heroic, full-length figure of Jefferson executed by the American sculptor, Rudolph Evans. On four panels along the sides of the interior rotunda are inscribed passages from his writings expressing his convictions of personal liberty and religious freedom and the obligation of the government to promote human progress, as well as paragraphs from the Declaration of Independence.

When all government, domestic and foreign, in little as in great things, shall be drawn to Washington as the center of all power, it will render powerless the checks provided of one government or another, and will become as venal and oppressive as the government from which we separated.

THOMAS JEFFERSON, 1821

Our Government is now taking so steady a course as to show by what road it will pass to destruction, to wit: by consolidation (i.e., centralisation) and then corruption, its necessary consequence.

The Letters of Thomas Jefferson

"We the people of the United States, in order to form a more perfect union, establish justice, insure domestic tranquility, provide for the common defense, promote the general welfare, and secure the blessings of liberty to ourselves and our posterity, do ordain and establish this Constitution for the United States of America."

(*We the people* were to promote the general welfare, not the Federal Government.)

*　　*　　*

These words, from the preamble to the Constitution, are plain American talk. There is no mistaking their meaning. The eternal truths they embody, the ceaseless striving for peace and happiness which they express, have made them immortal.

The usual words of greeting uttered and printed at this holiday season are as infinitely varied as language itself. But the net of all of them is the same. We all wish each other well. What, then, is the most practical and the most heartfelt way to convey this wish?

To one American it seems that in the fifty-two words of the above preamble is to be found the distilled wisdom of the ages—the aims and the ends of the good life as men and women of good-will wish it for one and all.

Held high where all may see them at all times, let these words be told and retold, dramatized and made

graphic to our children and those who follow, so that
they may cherish these aims, fight for these ends, and
win a greater share of these blessings than man has ever
before been granted on earth.

E. F. Hutton, "New Year, 1958," December 31, 1957;
                                    Palm Beach *Post*

PLACES OF REFLECTION

The Southwest is, in a manner of speaking, the Holy Land of America: the site of our most ancient memory, the scene of a human past which antedates ourselves. The beliefs that have impelled mankind to greatness have come always out of lonely places. Whatever America is or has been, the Southwest has been and is; it is the physical and spiritual heart of America. We know that freedom can be found only on a new soil. The Southwest, despite its age, is always new. This section has a particular meaning for every American: it sometimes shows itself as a simple longing for the soil, for the untrammeled life of nature; or the lure may be a passion for discovery—of places of the past, of treasures underground. It is the inexpressible loneliness and silence of the land around it. Here is the place of reflection where people seem to find themselves.

GREEN PEYTON, *America's Heartland: The Southwest;*
University of Oklahoma Press, 1948.

Innumerable historic landmarks and memorials and scenic shrines reward the visitor to that half-continent of lavish abundance and unhampered freedom. Everywhere, too, there has been the elemental struggle: the way of the land is still man against nature, sometimes a violent, terrifying nature—drought and dust, floods and "twisters," scorching sun and killing cold—periodic visitations which merely interrupt the people's progress and resourcefulness. And finally there is beauty—wild, rampant, breathtaking beauty beyond imagining, enriching the soul and ennobling the mind—and wonder—which Goethe called "the highest faculty to which man can attain"—leading to humility and gratitude and peace.

Texas is a national shrine in itself—as big as all outdoors, or almost, and oil, oil everywhere. It embraces a land area equal to that of New England, New York, New Jersey, Pennsylvania, and Illinois combined. Its turbulent history covers four centuries of life under six national flags. Its name derives from the word *tejas,* meaning "friendly;" and it became the twenty-eighth state to be admitted into the Union.

Its own particular shrine is the Alamo, a low, gray chapel-fortress of San Antonio's De Bexar Mission—in whose defense in 1836, against the invading Mexicans, the entire garrison of 188 Anglo-Americans perished, including Davy Crockett and Big Jim Bowie. Elsewhere throughout the city the influence of the Spanish conquistadors, *padres,* and early settlers still persists. One of the city's distinctive charms is the San Antonio River, so winding in its unhurried, meandering course that forty-two bridges must span it through the business and residential districts. Near Houston, the San Jacinto Memorial shaft marks the victory of General Sam Houston's meager forces over a superior Mexican army under Santa Anna, a battle which won for Texas her independence and freed from Mexican domination a third of the United States. The adjacent museum traces the development of the state from its discovery in 1519 to the Civil War. At El Paso, or El Paso Norte, as it was first called—the Pass of

the North from Mexico—six striking murals by T. J. Kittle-
son adorn the courthouse walls bearing the legend: "O path
of the North! Now the old giants are gone; we little men
live where heroes once walked the inviolate earth."

Arizona, fifth in size of all the states, is next to youngest,
having been admitted into the Union in 1912. The *Arizona
Guide Book* calls it "a land of extremes, of contrasts, of
surprises, of contradictions; a land that is never to be under-
stood but always to be loved by sons and daughters sprung
from such a diversity of origins, animated by such a diversity
of motives and ideals, that generations must pass before they
can ever fully understand each other."

Nature has given Arizona one of its brightest crown
jewels—the Grand Canyon of the Colorado, a shrine of the
ages sixty-five million years old. This enormous fissure, two
hundred miles long and a mile deep, defies attempts at description with words and brush, and it has been ranked by
many eyewitnesses as the most sublime spectacle in all the
world: "a constantly changing sample of eternity"; "a
complete course in geology, a botanical garden, an arche-
ological museum, a zoo." John Muir, the naturalist, said
of it that "it seems a gigantic statement for even nature to
make." The many-splendored gorge has been more often
painted than any other American scene.

A plan to build a million-dollar church near the edge
of the south rim of the Grand Canyon in Grand Canyon
National Park has alarmed a good many church-going, God-
fearing people who feel that such a structure would be an
anomaly at a spot where no man-made buildings could
possibly improve upon one of the most awesome sights of
nature.

The state points with pride to its sixteen National Monu-
ments commemorating scenes and events and relics of its
varied past: Casa Grande, Saguaro, Tumacacori, the Painted
Desert, the Petrified Forest, Montezuma Castle, San Xavier
Mission, Kaibab National Forest, the Madonna of the Trail,
Cochise Memorial Park, Canyon de Chelly Monument. And

the dramatic, haunting Apache Trail, winding its tortuous way into breathtaking Fish Creek Canyon; the Museum of Northern Arizona at Flagstaff, with its unusual displays which tell the whole story of the region's land and its people from prehistoric times to the present; the Arizona-Sonora Desert Museum just outside Tucson, an outdoor interpretive center where visitors may see at first hand the flora and fauna of the great open spaces, and where one encounters this touching epitaph on the headstone over the grave of a mountain lion who came to be beloved by all who knew him:

I freely give all sights and sounds of nature I have known to those who have the grace to enjoy not man-made materialism but God-made beauty—

The magnificent Arizona sunsets I have watched from my enclosure, I bequeath to all who see not only with their eyes but with their hearts—

To humans who are tired, worried or discouraged, I bequeath the silence, majesty and peace of our great American desert—

To those who walk the trails, I bequeath the early morning voices of the birds and the glory of the flowering desert in the springtime—

To the children who have enjoyed seeing me, hearing me purr, and watching me turn my somersaults, I offer the precious gift of laughter and joy. The world so needs these things—

And lastly, I bequeath my own happy spirit, and affection for others, to all who may remember me and my museum where for three years, I did my best to show people that I truly liked them.

New Mexico, fourth-largest state in area, is perhaps the richest in historical incident, representing a background of four centuries under Indian, Spanish, Mexican, and American cultures, still in many respects a frontier, as it has been since Coronado came. Santa Fe—the Royal City of the Holy Faith of St. Francis, founded in 1609—has been a capital continuously for more than three hundred years, its ancient streets and brown adobe houses teeming with great deeds and lasting memories. The Palace of the Governors contains the Museum of New Mexico and the library with rare editions, and is fashioned in the style of Pueblo construction.

In Cimarron, Buffalo Bill organized his Wild West show, rounding up Indians and pinto ponies. Up a canyon of the west fork of the Gila River, accessible only on foot or on horseback, is the Gila Cliff Dwellings National Monument, a community marking America's "first apartment houses." Taos, the city 7,000 feet up in the Sangre de Cristo Mountains, has colorful fiesta celebrations. The Taos Indian dances are noted for their beauty and precision, and its Society of Artists attracts nation-wide interest and attention to the charm of New Mexico. At Gallup is held the nation's biggest powwow, where Navajos and Cheyennes, Pawnees and Utes, together with members of some twenty-five other Indian tribes foregather for an annual Inter-Tribal Ceremonial around the Lyon Memorial Park.

President Franklin Pierce appointed General James Gadsden, United States Minister to Mexico, to negotiate, in 1853, a treaty for the purchase of some 45,000 square miles of Mexico's lands lying south of the Gila River and between the Colorado and the Rio Grande. Known as the Gadsden Purchase, the transaction involved $10,-000,000! In this raw country forts were built to protect ranchers and farmers and miners; stage coaches rolled crazily over the miles between St. Louis, Tucson and San Francisco; segments of the population of Eastern cities were breaking away and following Horace Greeley's familiar exhortation—"Go west, young man, go west." The wonder is that the men and women had the vision, the stamina and the bravery to have accomplished what they did.

BERNICE COSULICH, *Tucson;*
University of Arizona Press.

Americans possess no state church, no landed interest in the European sense, no squire, no parson, no aura of antiquity, no really distinct middle class, no imperial pride. But they retain the best written Constitution in the world, the safest division of powers, the widest diffusion of property, the strongest sense of common interest, the most prosperous economy, an elevated moral and intellectual tradition, and a spirit of resolute self-reliance unequaled in modern times.

RUSSELL KIRK, *The Conservative Mind;*
Henry Regnery Co., 1953.

The passion for local history is nationwide; it is *Everyman's* history. . . . In this year of mounting global stress, when to the general historian it seems that the Republic and what it stands for in the world lives from day to day in mortal peril, one might think that the American people would have little time for local history, regional, state, city or town. Yet never has there been such public interest in its support, such scholarly endeavor in its pursuit. When the whole world is threatened with an explosion of civilization in the atomic age, we turn instinctively to preserve the imprints of our local ways of life, liberty and the pursuit of happiness. . . . By competent studies of little American communities like this one, scholars are replowing the base and marking out the contours of our Republic. The general historian of the future must stand on this revived base and follow these smaller contours if he is to feel and portray the real American heritage.

SAMUEL F. BEMIS,
reviewing *Mirror to America* by James D. Squires;
published by the Village of New London, N.H.

THE SACRED SOIL

There is many a boy here today who looks on war as all glory; but, boys, it is all hell. You can bear this warning voice to generations yet to come. I am sick and tired of war and look upon it with horror. Its glory is all moonshine. It is only those who have never fired a shot nor heard the shrieks and groans of the wounded who cry aloud for blood, more vengeance, more desolation.
GEN. WILLIAM TECUMSEH SHERMAN, in an address at the G.A.R. Convention at Columbus, Ohio, August, 1880.

The battleground of Gettysburg is soil that will remain forever sacred, a dedicated place that witnessed the beginning of the end of a bloody civil war and a nation's fresh start toward unity and destiny. Here was a terrible three-day drama in which men surpassed themselves.

Bruce Catton, the eminent Civil War authority, has described the abiding significance of this hallowed shrine in a memorable passage: "What we hope to be, what we can yet bring forth on this continent, somehow dates from this

97

place. The park and the monuments and the thronging memories mean something beyond victory and defeat. The old sectional antagonisms fall away. What was lost by all of us, what was won here, was won by all of us. It offers to the visitor deep memories that go back into the purple twilight of the American story."

History has it that partly in the hope of winning foreign recognition, partly to encourage dissention and appeasement in the North, Gen. Robert E. Lee elected to carry the war to the enemy. Early in June, 1863, the Army of Northern Virginia began moving down the Shenandoah Valley.

A chance contact at Gettysburg of a part of the Confederate command of Gen. A. P. Hill with Buford's Union Cavalry division drew both forces into the town. With the battle thus joined, the Confederates met with an initial success by driving the Federal forces back to Cemetery Hill and Culp's Hill, while their own men occupied Seminary Ridge.

Gettysburg was won and lost on the second day of the three-day clash of arms when Longstreet failed to take strategic Little Round Top, from which vantage point he could have enfiladed the entire Union position; instead, he reluctantly attacked the strong Union center. When the long, gray lines of southern troops led by Pickett's division approached Cemetery Ridge, they were mercilessly mowed down by musket and artillery fire, only half a company succeeding in reaching the crest. Lee retired west of Sharpsburg, where the flooded Potomac blocked his retreat; but when Gen. Meade procrastinated in pressing his advantage, Lee made good his escape into Virginia.

The Gettysburg battleground was left a sea of carnage: the Confederate losses having been 3,900 killed and 24,000 wounded and missing; the Union losses, 3,100 killed and 20,000 wounded or missing. After the early auspicious victories of the southern forces, Gettysburg marked the turning point in the fortunes of the Confederacy. Despite the raw courage and supreme effort of his troops, Lee's offensive strength had been dealt a mortal blow and his reckless strategy thwarted thereafter. Northern manpower, finances, communication, supplies, and resources were to assert themselves. Lincoln, meanwhile, had finally found the military leader he was so desperately in need of, in the person of Gen. Grant, whose success at Vicksburg gave the Union forces control of the Mississippi River from Illinois to New Orleans and cut the Confederacy completely in two.

In November, following the battle, the Gettysburg National Military Cemetery was dedicated—the scene of Lincoln's memorable address, perhaps the summit of American eloquence. Edward Everett, one of the nation's renowned orators, had preceded Lincoln with a lengthy summation of the military strategy. He was later to write the President, "I should be glad if I could flatter myself that I came as near the central idea of the occasion in two hours as you did in two minutes."

Fourscore and seven years ago our forefathers brought forth on this continent a new nation, conceived in liberty, and dedicated to the proposition that all men are created equal. Now we are engaged in a great civil war, testing whether that nation, or any nation so conceived and so dedicated, can long endure. We are met on a great battlefield of that war. We have come to dedicate a portion of that field as a final resting-place of those who here gave their lives that that nation might live. It is altogether fitting and proper that we should do this. But in a larger sense, we cannot dedicate, we cannot consecrate, we cannot hallow this ground. The brave men, living and dead, who struggled here, have consecrated it far above our poor power to add or detract. The world will little note, nor long remember, what we say here; but it can never forget what they did here. It is for us, the living, rather to be dedicated here to the unfinished work which they who fought here have thus far so nobly advanced. It is rather for us to be here dedicated to the great task remaining before us, that from these honored dead we take increased devotion to that cause for which they gave the last full measure of devotion; that we here highly resolve that these dead shall not have died in vain; that this nation, under God, shall have a new birth of freedom, and that government of the people, by the people, for the people, shall not perish from the earth.

THE CONESTOGA

The vision that the world is waiting is
The same that traced its way in wagon-tracks
Across empurpled plain and precipice,
And whispered in the star-lit tamaracks
Where travelers told of freedom of the West
Around the fires of hopeful bivouacs:
The vision of a mighty purpose, pressed
By all the peoples of the earth, to make
The hidden truth within them manifest;
And as this continent was free to take,
And thus awoke the hope of all mankind.
So now, in hope, we hear the future break
On the unsovereigned beaches of the mind.

RUSSELL W. DAVENPORT, *My Country;*
Simon and Schuster, 1955.

From a blacksmith shop in a Pennsylvania hamlet they
recently wheeled out a hundred-and-thirty-year-old Cones-

toga wagon, all gaily painted—the underbody blue, the upper parts red—complete with its ancient gear and fittings. A hitch of six Belgian drays drew the still-sturdy prairie schooner from Lancaster to Wheeling, West Virginia, to commemorate the first manufacture, entirely by hand, of a rumbling old English "rolling cart" about the year 1750.

This was the predecessor of the so-called "vehicles of empire," not many of which are still able to roll; but each one extant is an American shrine in itself, the embodiment of all that went to make up one of the great migrations of history. In this reckless venture there were privation and death, drama and tumult, romance, tragedy, and success. Disdainful of hardship and danger, these pioneer sodbusters, farmers, prospectors, and homesteaders set up their tents on the plains or on the mountainsides, or along the perilous rivers, sustained by vision and faith and courage—the virtues that were to throw open half a continent. Nor were the men alone in these bold undertakings: without the resourcefulness and self-reliance of their women, who eagerly accepted the challenge, the westward stream of American history would have been an abortive thing, turned back at the first river barrier, the grim advance faltering at the foot of the first mountain range.

"For history reminds us that the American West of the early eighteen-hundreds was a land of rumor, known in its parts by a few trappers and explorers, known as a whole by no one. The sources of its great rivers, the extent of its mountain ranges, were a matter of fairly vague conjecture by geographers who often depicted the continental features as they 'must be' rather than as they were. The covered-wagon trail was recorded as being at once a hardship and wonderment, of freedom and movement, which was to become lodged forever in the lexicon, legend and consciousness of the American people."

SCHMITT AND BROWN,
The Settler's West; Scribner's, 1955.

These dedicated crusaders must have been animated

with the conviction that life were a petty thing unless moved
by an indomitable urge to extend its boundaries: "Only in
proportion as we are desirous of living more do we live
really. In times of fulness of life our horizon expands, moving in unison almost with our breathing. When the horizon
stiffens, it is because it has become fossilized and we are
getting old."

And so the Conestoga wagon can rightly be regarded as
the cradle of westward expansion—one of the most distinc-
tively American devices of all our transportation history.
Following in the wake of the pack horse and the pony express, it did the pioneering for the canal boat and the railroad. It first came into general use on the overland routes
across the Alleghenies about 1783, sometimes moving in solitary grandeur, sometimes in caravans stretching out for
miles. Taking its name, in all likelihood, from a small tri-
butary of the Susquehanna River in Pennsylvania, the Conestoga was first pulled by oxen, later by Missouri mules,
eventually by horses.

An adaptation of the English road wagon, the Conestoga
was a huge structure, heavily built, with broad-rimmed,
medium-sized front wheels and much larger rear wheels so
that the load might be thrown forward and give a more
efficient drawbar pull. The wagon bed was higher at either
end than in the middle and was topped by a dull-white
canvas cloth. It was tightly enough built to stay afloat during
brief fordings, and of stout enough planking to turn aside
the low-velocity bullets from Indian guns. Such was the
crude conveyance that opened up the rich new world beyond
the Rockies and made America the land of opportunity for
a whole generation.

Come, stand in history's wagon tracks at Scotts Bluff,
deeply rutted into the red clay of the Oregon Trail, little
changed since the wheels of the covered wagons cut them
a hundred years ago. Here, at this welcome landmark, the
pioneers rested, fixed the wagons and saw to the seed-corn

. . . for ahead lay the challenging Rockies and the scalp-lifting Indians who threatened the way to the fertile Northwest. There's enough pioneer history at Scotts Bluff to keep a small boy wide-eyed for days. *This was Indian country* . . . the warpath of the Sioux, Arapahoe and Cheyenne. In the frontier museum, you'll see relics of the Trail, vivid dioramas, paintings by a pioneer artist that bring alive the terror of an Indian raid, the whip of a sudden prairie squall, the thundering hooves of the buffalo herd. Not far away is old Fort Laramie where the U.S. Cavalry galloped out to rescue ambushed wagon trains. Scotts Bluff and the wagon tracks have been preserved as reminders of the fearless determination that pushed back our frontiers. It's good to know *this courage still pulses strong in the hearts of Americans.*

From *Sinclair Oil Corporation*'s
American Conservation Series; 1958.

To the frontier, the American intellect owes its striking characteristics. That coarseness and strength, combined with acuteness and inquisitiveness; that practical and inventive turn of mind, quick to find expedients; that masterful grasp of material things, lacking in the artistic but powerful to effect great ends; that restless, nervous energy; that dominant individualism, working for good and for evil, and withal that buoyancy and exuberance which comes with freedom—these are the traits called out by the existence of the frontier.

FREDERICK JACKSON TURNER,
The Significance of the Frontier in American History;
Henry Holt and Company, 1920.

"The cowards never started—and the weak died along the way."

CALIFORNIA AND BEYOND

The pioneers who had aided in the conquest of the Far West—the Santa Fe traders, the mountain men, the farmers who followed the Oregon and California trails westward, the Mormons in their desert Zion, the forty-niners, the prospectors who dug their gold in remote mining camps—had founded not one but a galaxy of empires, scattered widely over a vast and distant land. In the future new and equally bold frontiersmen were to follow the trails they had blazed, but they were to be borne westward on rattling railroad cars, and they were to carry with them the artifacts of a machine civilization. Man had begun his battle against nature with only his hands and his brain to aid him; man was to continue that battle with such efficient tools that only thirty years later this continent had been conquered and all the Far West subjected to the elevating forces of civilization.

RAY ALLEN BILLINGTON,
The Far Western Frontier; Harper's, 1952.

California was named by Cortés in 1535; Juan Rodríguez Cabrillo discovered the southern coast in 1542; Sir Francis Drake, in search of new lands and treasures for the Crown, sailed his ship, the *Golden Hind,* into Drake's Bay near San Francisco in 1579, accepting from the Indians sovereignty over the territory, calling it Nova Albion—New England. He was the first Englishman to land in California. The state's eighteen national forests comprise one-fifth of its area, and within its boundaries there are nineteen historical monuments. The one honoring Cabrillo, on Point Loma overlooking the city of San Diego, is said to be visited by more persons each year than any other of the nation's national shrines. There are forty-one peaks in its mountain ranges that are more than 10,000 feet in height, while Death Valley, 280 feet below sea level, is the lowest point in the United States, and, in summer, one of the hottest places on earth, with temperatures as high as 134 degrees in the shade. It was also made a National Monument, in 1933.

The great legacy of the Spaniards is, of course, the California missions, twenty-one in number, scattered at intervals along the Camino Real, or King's Highway, from San Diego to Sonomo. Among the most revered Catholic shrines in the nation, their history goes back to 1769, when Father Junípero Serra, head of the Franciscan missionaries, set out to bring Christianity to the Indians. Neglected and allowed to deteriorate when Mexico seized church properties in 1832, the missions have been substantially restored to their original state—a Spanish-Moorish style, for the most part, of adobe construction with tile roofs. Those of San Juan Capistrano, San Carlos Barromeo, Santa Barbara—"the Queen of Missions"—San Miguel, San Juan Bautista, San Luis Obispo, San Gabriel Arcangel, are considered to be among the most noteworthy examples.

"Spread out along some six hundred miles of California's southern coast," writes Cornelius Vanderbilt, Jr., in *The Living Past of America,* "is the fabulous chain of missions

which constitutes one of the most interesting historical preservations of the country. Regardless of the importance of
these missions, the influence of the Franciscan Fathers who
founded and conducted them, and their impact on American
history and culture, this largest single segment of America's
living past always had and continues to have a world of
romantic appeal to Americans."

Captain John A. Sutter, a Swiss adventurer, established
a trading post and fort on the present site of Sacramento,
and in partnership with one James W. Marshall set about
to build a sawmill a short distance away. In 1848, Marshall
came upon what proved to be the first fabulous golden flakes
in the millrace and made the discovery that was to rock the
world. The news spread like wildfire, and the headlong trek
was on. Promoters, explorers, gamblers, fakers, flocked to
the scene from far and near by whatever means of travel
were available, dropping whatever they may have been
engaged in, to stake their all on sharing in the sudden wealth
of the new-found El Dorado, to the refrain of—

> Oh! California,
> That's the land for me;
> I'm off for Sacramento
> With my washbowl on my knee.

A State Park has taken over the discovery site at the
town of Coloma, and a museum there contains important
memorabilia of the frantic gold-rush period.

For more than three centuries the West attracted restless and curious white men. First were the Spanish Explorers, who searched avidly but unsuccessfully for the
fabled Cities of Cibola, only to find that they were the
seven adobe pueblos of Zuñi, gilded by sunlight. They
became a symbol of the lure which beckoned men and
made them crazy; while they searched and killed, found
and lost the silver and gold. Sometimes the frantic quest

made them millionaires one day, paupers the next. But even when they lost, their eyes kept searching the sandy river banks and the rocky sides of mountains for the "strike" they knew was ahead of them; and as they grew older, the glitter grew brighter and their efforts became more determined. Tomorrow was another day.

MURIEL S. WOLLE,
Bonanza Trail: Ghost Towns and Mining Camps
of the West;
Indiana University Press, 1953.

After Meriwether Lewis and William Clark had carried the Stars and Stripes from Missouri to the shores of the Pacific, they made camp for the winter of 1805–6 at Fort Clatsop near the mouth of the Columbia River, at Astoria, Oregon—named for a tribe of coastal Indians. The site is under consideration for another national shrine: it was there that American conquest of the West began; it was the first settlement by Americans along the Pacific seaboard; it was the first building to house white persons in the Pacific Northwest. The rebuilt version of the first of all American homes in the West may well become one of America's most popular historic sites, symbolizing, as it does, the nation's transcontinental beginnings.

The man of the Old West was not a sensitive creature, and he found it perfectly possible to keep a clear conscience while he defied proprietors and quitrents, squatted wherever he found a fertile valley, and massacred the Indians who protested at his high handedness. His Calvinism lay broad and deep and made him look upon God as a business partner and a tribal deity who regarded with favor self-reliance and direct action. There is a story of a Western preacher—a Scotch-Irishman—who during the Revolution opened a recruiting meeting with this remarkable prayer: "Lord God, if Thou art unwilling by

divine grace to assist us, do stand aside and let us fight
it out!"

LELAND DEWITT BALDWIN, *The Meaning of America;*
University of Pittsburgh Press, 1955.

For the measure of America's greatness, read the historians. They are the reviewers, the provers. Expertly they
search and sift the record, keep the check-up of a nation,
test the validity of an ideal and give the weight and
blood count of a heritage. But for the heartbeat, go to
the people. To be transported into the past, raw and free
of the processing of later-day handlers, to be swept off-
page into life as our forebears lived it—for this we must
turn to those who wrote, at the time, of the America
they saw and touched and breathed.

JOSEF and DOROTHY BERGER, *Diary of America;*
Simon and Schuster, 1957.

SHRINES OF REMEMBRANCE

For these men [in the Confederate Army] believed in
something. They counted life a light thing to lay down
in the faith they bore. They were terrible in battle. They
were generous in victory. They rose up from defeat to
fight again, and while they lived they were formidable.
There were not enough of them; that is all.

JOHN W. THOMASON, JR.,
Speaking of the Confederate Army.

Every man's life belongs to his country, and no man has
a right to refuse it when his country calls for it.
UNION GEN. JOHN A. LOGAN

When this leader of one of the Union armies spoke these
words in a cemetery at Carbondale, Illinois, in April, 1866,
he probably chose the time and place to inaugurate and consecrate Memorial—or Decoration—Day, which has been solemnly celebrated on the thirtieth day of May each year in all

but a few states since its first national observance in 1868.

This solemn tribute was first suggested in 1866 by three women of Columbus, Mississippi, who decorated the graves of Confederate soldiers there and at the same time laid flowers on the graves of Union soldiers buried in the cemetery. At the instance of his wife, John A. Logan, as Chief of Staff, issued an official order shortly thereafter proclaiming Memorial Day an annual ceremonial, and the custom has since become general throughout the country.

Americans make this annual pilgrimage of honor, gratitude, and supplication to pay homage to their war dead; and to pray, as Abraham Lincoln did in his letter written in 1864 to Mrs. Bixby, who had lost five sons in the civil conflict: "May our heavenly Father assuage the anguish of your bereavement and leave you only the cherished memory of the loved and lost and the solemn pride that must be yours to have laid so costly a sacrifice upon the altar of freedom."

One hundred national military cemeteries dot the land, from Arlington on the Potomac to the Golden Gate, from St. Augustine in Florida to Custer, Montana; in Honolulu; Mexico City; San Juan, Puerto Rico; Sitka, Alaska, as well as many other burial grounds elsewhere around the world: "In these temples, as in the hearts of the people for whom they saved the Republic, the memory of these gallant men is enshrined forever."

> The muffled drum's sad roll has beat
> The soldier's last tattoo!
> No more on life's parade shall meet
> The brave and fallen few.
> On Fame's eternal camping ground
> Their silent tents are spread,
> And Glory guards with solemn round
> The bivouac of the dead.
>
> .   .   .   .
>
> Rest on, embalmed and sainted dead,
> Dear is the blood you gave—

No impious footstep here shall tread
   The herbage of your grave.
Nor shall your glory be forgot
   While fame her record keeps,
Or honor points the hallowed spot
   Where Valor proudly sleeps.

The Bivouac of the Dead;
Theodore O'Hara, Confederate Soldier, 1820-1867.

The Grand Army of the Republic has answered the last roll call, with the death of its sole survivor, Albert Woolson, at the incredible age of 109, he having outlived 2,675,000 soldiers who wore the blue, and all but three of the veterans who wore the Confederate gray. Woolson enlisted at seventeen in the First Minnesota Volunteer Heavy Artillery, Company C. Under a special privilege granted to underage soldiers, he cast his vote for Lincoln in the Presidential election of 1864. He had posed as model of the memorial statue honoring the Union forces which stands in the Gettysburg National Military Park. Something essentially American has gone forever; a stirring chapter in our history has been finished.

As it has been well said, "The strength of this country is in the spirit of its manhood. It springs from the earth and dwells in the air of a nation determined to know its ancient liberty. The stillness in which lie our fighting men is that of victory, and so it has always been from the days of the Revolution—through the struggles of 1812—1846—1861—1898—1917—1941—until in 1950 our handcuffed formations were restrained in Korea and kept from the expected fulfillment that was in their grasp!"

It has lately been suggested that this most solemn of our national holidays may well take on a wider significance. Thus the New York *Times* has given this editorial expression: "Memorial Day can be our finest holiday if we make it also a Day of Remembrance. Our dead belong to all of us, just as that for which they died is the heritage of all. We can

pay tribute to all those who have their own gift to that
heritage without in the least taking away from the special
place that belongs to the men who have died in conflict.
Theirs was the supreme sacrifice, but we can honor those
also whose place has been less conspicuous but whose gift
may have been no less enduring. In every field of human
endeavor—parenthood, teaching, science, medicine, nursing,
research, the ministry—there can be special remembrance for
all those who have been the pioneers. They lacked the plainly
marked guideposts that we use without even thinking. They
broke the new ground. We are forever in their debt."

War is a temporary adoption, by men of the character
of wild beasts, emulating their philosophy, rejoicing like
them in blood, and seeking, as with a lion's paw, to hold
an asserted right. The character of war is somewhat dis-
guised, in more recent days, by the scale and knowledge
which it employs; it is, however, still the same, made
more destructive by the genius and intellect which have
been delegated to its servants.
CHARLES SUMNER, "The Grandeur of Nations,"
Oration delivered July 4, 1845

There will always be the sound of thunder and there will
always be wars, death, ruin and calamity in the affairs
of men and nations, until they enter into the tranquility
of God.
LAO-TSE, Chinese philosopher

AMERICAN IMMORTALS

The true glory of a nation is an intelligent, honest, industrious people. The civilization of a people depends on their individual character; and a constitution which is not the outgrowth of this character is not worth the parchment on which it is written. You look in vain in the past for a single instance where the people have preserved their liberties after their individual character was lost. The true glory of a nation is the living temple of a loyal, industrious, upright people. . . . Would you see the image of true national glory, I would show you villages where the crown and glory of the people are in common schools, where the voice of prayer goes heaven-

ward, where the people have that most priceless gift—
faith in God.

E. P. WHIPPLE, "The True Glory of a Nation" in
1000 American Things, compiled by Hugh Graham; Spencer Press; distributed by Hawthorn
Books, 1957.

The American institution of Halls of Fame has become
of incalculable value in helping us to reach a fuller appreciation of the richness of our past and pursue a more dili-
gent exploration of our background. Of first importance
among these shrines of achievement is the Hall of Fame for
Great Americans on the campus of New York University
on University Heights in the Bronx. This 630-foot open-air
colonnade, originated by Dr. Henry W. MacCracken, Chan-
cellor of the University, designed by Stanford White and
built in 1900 with funds contributed by the late Helen
Gould Shepard, with its memorial tablets and bronze busts,
is a significant collection of portrait sculpture as well as a
unique presentation of American history and biography.

Any person born in the United States or whose work
has been thoroughly identified with this country over a long
period of time—and who has been dead twenty-five years or
more—is eligible for enrollment. One hundred and fifty
memorial niches have been provided, of which eighty-six
have thus far been filled. Supplementing the twenty-nine
persons of great distinction originally selected, fifty-seven
names have since been added. Elections are held every five
years, from nominations from the public; candidates are
screened by a panel of prominent citizens from every state
in the Union, and are voted upon by a College of Electors.
No more than seven nominees may be chosen at any one
election.

The roster as at present constituted is a roll call of men
and women from varied walks of life, conspicuous for their
outstanding contributions to America since its beginning as
a free nation:

John Adams (1735-1826), statesman, second President
John Quincy Adams (1767-1848), statesman, sixth President
Louis Agassiz (1807-73), naturalist
Susan B. Anthony (1820-1906), woman-suffrage advocate
John James Audubon (1785-1851), ornithologist, artist
George Bancroft (1800-1891), historian
Henry Ward Beecher, (1813-87), clergyman
Alexander Graham Bell (1847-1922), inventor of telephone
Daniel Boone (1734-1820), pioneer, explorer
Edwin Thomas Booth (1833-93), actor
Phillips Brooks (1835-93), Episcopal bishop
William Cullen Bryant (1794-1878), poet and editor
William Ellery Channing (1780-1842), Unitarian clergyman
Rufus Choate (1799-1859), lawyer, orator
Henry Clay (1777-1852), statesman
Samuel L. Clemens (1835-1910), Mark Twain; author, humorist
Stephen Grover Cleveland (1837-1908), statesman, 22nd and 24th President
James Fenimore Cooper (1789-1851), novelist
Peter Cooper (1791-1883), manufacturer, philanthropist
Charlotte S. Cushman (1816-76), actress
James B. Eads (1820-1887), engineer, inventor
Jonathan Edwards (1703-58), Congregational theologian
Ralph Waldo Emerson (1803-82), poet, essayist
David Glasgow Farragut (1801-70), admiral
Stephen Collins Foster (1826-64), song writer, composer
Benjamin Franklin (1706-90), statesman, scientist, philosopher
Robert Fulton (1765-1815), inventor, steamboat builder
Josiah Willard Gibbs (1790-1861), physicist
William C. Gorgas (1854-1920), surgeon-general, United States Army; sanitary officer, Panama Canal
Ulysses Simpson Grant (1822-85), soldier, statesman, 18th President

Asa Gray (1810-88), botanist

Alexander Hamilton (1757-1804), statesman, first Secretary of Treasury

Nathaniel Hawthorne (1804-64), novelist, storyteller

Joseph Henry (1797-1878), physicist, instituted weather reports

Patrick Henry (1736-99), statesman, Revolutionary leader

Oliver Wendell Holmes (1809-94), man of letters

Mark Hopkins (1802-87), educator, lecturer

Elias Howe (1819-67), inventor of sewing machine

Washington Irving (1783-1859), writer of essays, short stories

Andrew Jackson (1767-1845), statesman, seventh President

Thomas Jonathan (Stonewall) Jackson (1824-63), Confederate general

Thomas Jefferson (1743-1826), statesman, third President

John Paul Jones (1747-92), naval officer

James Kent (1763-1847), jurist

Sidney Lanier (1842-81), poet

Robert Edward Lee (1807-70), military officer, educator

Abraham Lincoln (1809-65), statesman, 16th President

Henry W. Longfellow (1807-82), poet

James Russell Lowell (1819-91), poet

Mary Lyon (1797-1849), educator

James Madison (1751-1836), statesman, fourth President

Horace Mann (1796-1859), educator

John Marshall (1755-1835), jurist, Chief Justice

Matthew F. Maury (1806-73), oceanographer

Maria Mitchell (1818-89), astronomer

James Monroe (1758-1831), statesman, fifth President

Samuel F. B. Morse (1791-1872), inventor of telegraph

William T. G. Morton (1819-68), dentist

John Lothrop Motley (1814-77), historian

Simon Newcomb (1835-1909), astronomer

Thomas Paine (1737-1809), philosopher

Alice Freeman Palmer (1855-1902), educator, historian
Francis Parkman (1823-93), historian
George Peabody (1795-1869), merchant, art patron
William Penn (1644-1718), colonizer
Edgar Allan Poe (1809-49), poet, story teller
Walter Reed (1851-1902), surgeon
Theodore Roosevelt (1858-1919), statesman, 25th President
Augustus Saint-Gaudens (1848-1907), sculptor
William Tecumseh Sherman (1820-91), U. S. Army commander
Joseph Story (1779-1845), jurist
Harriet Beecher Stowe (1811-96), author, abolitionist
Gilbert Charles Stuart (1755-1828), painter
Booker T. Washington (1856-1915), Negro educator, established Tuskegee Institute
George Washington (1732-1799), general, statesman, first President
Daniel Webster (1782-1852), statesman, orator
George Westinghouse (1864-1914), inventor of air brake for railway cars
James A. McNeill Whistler (1834-1903), painter—"Portrait of My Mother"
Walt Whitman (1819-92), poet, journalist
Eli Whitney (1765-1825), inventor of the cotton gin, system of interchangeable parts
John Greenleaf Whittier (1807-92), poet
Emma Willard (1787-1870), educator
Frances E. Willard (1839-98), reformer, leader in temperance movement
Roger Williams (1603-83), clergyman, founder of colony of Rhode Island
Thomas Woodrow Wilson (1856-1924), statesman, 28th President
Wilbur Wright (1867-1912), pioneer in aviation, patented flying machine

In Chicago's huge Merchandise Mart was established a few years ago by Joseph P. Kennedy, its owner, a Hall of Fame to immortalize outstanding American merchants whose distinguished contributions to merchandising have had a continuing and far-reaching impact on the national economy. Bronze sculptured busts four times life-size stand on the Mart's plaza, honoring seven distinguished figures of the retail world: Marshall Field, founder of Chicago's Marshall Field & Company; Edward A. Filene, of Filene's department store in Boston; George H. Hartford, first head of the Great Atlantic and Pacific Tea Company; Julius Rosenwald, of Sears, Roebuck and Company; John R. Wanamaker, founder of the Wanamaker Stores in Philadelphia and New York; Gen. Robert E. Wood, retired chairman of Sears, Roebuck and Company (the first living merchant to be chosen for the gallery) ; and Frank W. Woolworth, originator of the five-and-ten-cent store.

Another shrine of immortals is being readied in the reception room of the United States Senate wing of the Capitol to receive the portraits of the five most distinguished Solons, recently selected by a special senatorial committee, which will grace the five oval niches, unoccupied since the Capitol was completed in 1859. The five were chosen from the more than two thousand elected senators who have served during the 168-year history of the body; none living were eligible. Those honored are:

Henry Clay (1777-1852) , Kentucky Whig
John C. Calhoun (1782-1850) , South Carolina Democrat
Daniel Webster (1782-1852) , Massachusetts Whig
Robert La Follette (1855-1925) , Wisconsin Progressive
    Republican
Robert A. Taft (1889-1953) , Ohio Republican

A stately chamber in the Hall of Fame of the International College of Surgeons on Chicago's Lake Shore Drive is dedicated to the great men who have made epoch-making contributions to scientific progress, freedom from suffering, and the prolongation of life.

The addition of a decade and a half to the average man's tenure of life within half a century is an immense enrichment of the world. Even greater is the enrichment that comes of relief from anxiety, the intellectual and spiritual release, the more abundant flowering of man's powers that follows rescue from the tyranny of fear.
MARK SULLIVAN, *Our Times;* Vol. I., Scribner's, 1954.

History is what really happened, and it is what men have thought really happened; it is what men did, and the emotions that moved them while they were doing it. The lesson of history remains fluid; perhaps in the end it is nothing much more definite than the demonstration that human life is a many-splendored thing of infinite variety.

BRUCE CATTON in *American Heritage,*
The Magazine of History; James Parton, publisher.

THE SANCTUARY

One of the great meanings which the American land of promise held for its original settlers was an almost incomprehensible richness of endowment in wildlife. The first explorers, only a few brief centuries ago, recorded in their journals the wildlife paradise through which they traveled. What has happened to these resources of the continent is an epic of wanton waste and slaughter. Man is not going to survive on wildlife: there are too many humans and too little wildlife; but the latter can be protected and perpetuated if men so wish—which they do.

MICHAEL W. STRAUS, *Why Not Survive?;*
Simon and Schuster, 1955.

Americans are annually reminded by the National Wildlife Federation of the ever-continuing need for conservation and the necessity for stimulating the interest of young and old in our priceless natural environment. The "Save America's Wetlands" theme, augmented by the issuance of a series of thirty-six postage stamps in color portraying a variety of wild fowl, calls attention to the growing threat to such mysterious habitats as our swamps, bayous, marshes, and inland lakes by drainage, pollution, and selfish depredations.

At the southernmost corner of Florida, the Everglades National Park—twenty-eighth in the system and exceeded in extent only by the Yellowstone and the Mount McKinley reservations—is in the final stages of completion. The only subtropical national park in the United States, this fascinating sanctuary promises to become one of the few unspoiled parts of the recreational life of America—a timeless wilderness made available to hundreds of thousands of visitors every year with a minimum of discomfort and a maximum of hospitality in close proximity to the metropolitan center of Miami.

"The Everglades is all wild, from its regal royal palms to its fierce strangler figs; from its ruling alligators to the minute forms of life that are plucked up with every cupful of water from the swamp. Here is nature involved in internecine warfare, but vigorous in an inscrutable natural balance. The park is a zoo without cages, an aquarium without tanks, an unfenced botanical garden, and, most of all, a vast aviary. There is no other like it." (Hubert Saal, in *Town and Country*, January, 1957.)

Everglades Park is primarily a refuge where spectacular —and nearly extinct—species may live unmolested by the inroads of civilization, traversing their familiar haunts "on the wings of God's grace and beauty," over an area of a million and a half acres, much of which is under water most of the year. (Land must be filled in and built up above water level to provide sites for development and road construction.) Cruise boats are available, from which the bird rookeries can be studied along the mangrove waterways, where the bird-viewer and practiced photographer will encounter a profusion of rare specimens. A wide variety of birds, mammals, and reptiles, all threatened with extinction, are being given a chance of survival. The ivory-billed woodpecker is now all but extinct, and the rare seaside sparrow and the whooping crane—America's largest bird—are not often encountered elsewhere. Other species, happier in this Florida haven, are trumpeter swans, the great white heron, the wood ibis, roseate spoonbills, man-o'-war birds, ospreys, owls, short-tailed hawks, the seldom-seen egret, the Everglades kite. Among the reptiles, the American crocodile and the green turtle are making this their last stand. And unless something is done by the authorities, that tiny and historical animal— the Key deer—will not be around much longer in his Florida surroundings.

Thus does Everglades National Park stand as another barrier against private-interest groups that would plunder our remaining natural resources and appropriate the wealth of soil, water, timber, and wildlife to their own ends. Down at Cape Sable, at the southwestern edge of the park, a stone marks the grave of Guy M. Bradley, the late warden of the National Audubon Society, who in 1905 was killed while protecting birds from plume-hunters. His untimely death spurred the national movement in the interest of wildlife conservation.

The superintendent of this vast domain is Daniel Carter Beard, son of the master woodsman from whom a generation of American boys learned their woodcraft. "Millions of people," observes Mr. Beard, "are tremendously interested in these birds, animals and forests and in all the things we are trying to show them here. A generation of Americans have grown up in our time who have a better appreciation of wildlife and what it means than people had when *we* were growing up."

From the lookout tower, one may glimpse the Ten Thousand Islands and the countless shell mounds, which have raised the elevation of the land with clam and oyster shells, where the Indians lived for centuries. Along Halfway Creek are the remnants of man's unequal struggle with the wilderness—a church, a few homes and farms—all deserted and reclaimed by nature as its own. A chain of waterways takes a visitor among the distinctive flora and fauna and into a jungle of mangroves, which are believed to have drifted here hundred of years ago from the African coast to form thousands of our offshore islands.

It were well for all of us to bear in mind and put into practice America's Conservation Pledge: "I give my word of honor as an American to save and faithfully to defend from waste the natural resources of my country—its soil and minerals, its forests, waters and wildlife."

Song From the Everglades

Here in the Everglades, away from snow
And ice that blanket half a shivering world,
Swift wings of pink flamingos rise and flow
Along the warm blue winds. Hot lilies are curled
In petaled sleep as butterflies await
Their scarlet waking. Drifting, blind with sun,
Islands of hyacinths bear their trembling freight
Of shimmering purple. Till the day is done
Proud throats of wild birds lift into the sky
A stranger music than mortals could ever sing.
Lightly as pollen the hours drift away
In this lost heaven of eternal spring.

DANIEL WHITEHEAD HICKY

THE SYMBOL

Wildlife is one of those renewable resources that must be managed if we are to have continued benefits from it. The whole people have a common interest here. The enjoyment of wildlife and what goes with it are a part of our standard of living. People who concern themselves with the nation's resource problems are backing the wilderness idea in increasing numbers. They see the essential services that undisturbed lands can render; preservation of unique scenery, vegetation types, vanishing animal and bird life, recreation in the out-of-doors, educational and scientific uses. But the greatest appeal of wilderness probably is an elusive and esthetic one. Our natural areas are the last opportunity Americans will have to view their country as it once was. They are a brief glimpse of history, a last communion with the primitive.

DURWARD L. ALLEN, *Our Wildlife Legacy;*
Funk and Wagnalls Co., 1953.

The preservation of the Everglades National Park may well be the last refuge of the American bald eagle—our national symbol. This reclaimed kingdom harbors the largest number of this proud species now extant, and protection and vigilance are needed if they are to survive and multiply. Elsewhere throughout the United States this majestic bird is fast disappearing. Its extinction is due chiefly to the march of progress, the depletion of basic soil, water, and plant resources, and extensive logging operations that destroy many of the lofty perches where they nest and the fish and small mammals which they feed on. The weather has also been to blame, severe storms destroying many of their eggs, fledglings, and aeries, while trigger-happy hunters have probably accounted for a great number of them, perhaps mistaking them for large hawks.

John Kieran, the well-known naturalist and writer, in his *An Introduction to Birds* (Doubleday, 1950), observes that "while the Bald Eagle—the white head and tail feathers do not appear until the bird reaches maturity—has its faults, it is a bird of great dignity and noble bearing, with a wing-spread of more than thirty inches, and wonderful powers of flight. Bald eagles will engage in armed robbery, threatening lesser birds with their terrific talons and forcing them to yield up the food they may be taking off. They have been accused of carrying away and devouring little babies, but such stories are regarded as fairy tales. As the national bird of the United States, it has become famous in song and story."

The National Audubon Society has undertaken an extensive survey to ascertain how many of the bald eagle tribe may still be extant, and what measures will be needed to spare and protect them. Formerly the undisputed monarch of American skies, these great birds flew unmolested over the land in large numbers, their imposing aspect and shrill scream familiar to everyone. Today, students of birdlore reckon that less than a thousand of them may still be at large, most of them seeking asylum in the watery fastnesses of the Florida Everglades.

Having adopted the Declaration of Independence, the Continental Congress, in 1776, promptly proceeded to the execution of a design for a Great Seal for the young repub-lic—a design that would become part of our language and currency, the accepted symbol of "the United States of North America."

"We are now a nation," announced the Speaker, John Hancock, "and I am ready to hear you vote on the matter." But it was to be six years before "the matter" was finally resolved.

After protracted debate and lengthy consideration of various conceptions submitted to the several committees, the official heraldry was finally chosen—the work of one William Barton, a young Philadelphia artist well versed in heraldry. Familiar with the popularity of the eagle, from its place atop the standards of the Roman legions to its adop-tion in his own time, Barton incorporated the American eagle as its central symbol. Charles Thomson, secretary of the Congress, sketched out a shield on its breast, an olive branch and arrows in its talons—all circled by thirteen stars surrounded by clouds. This composite, with minor varia-tions, is the seal as it is today (as found, for instance, on the reverse face of a one-dollar bill).

The discussion found Benjamin Franklin in vigorous dis-sent, for he held the eagle to be "a bird of bad moral char-acter, who does not come by his living honestly, and is a rank coward." His own candidate for the place of honor in the insigne was either a rattlesnake or a wild turkey; but his eloquence was unavailing.

The people were quick to take the eagle as their own; china and chintz, draperies and bedspreads, wallpaper and floor-coverings, paneling and furniture, figureheads and fire marks, coins and postage stamps, glass and ceramics, soon displayed the spreading wings and defiant countenance as a mark of pride and distinction. The eagle became a personal emblem; there hovered over the hearths which displayed replicas the aura of liberty, a sense of security. Whether cast in the metal from molds or carved in wood, in miniature or of heroic size, in picture or needlecraft, the patriotic device belonged to the home much as a trusted companion or protector, a reminder of our privilege, our opportunity, our freedom, and our obligation. Although traditionally portrayed with a mien of fierceness, its attitude has been accepted as one of protection rather than of prey, of challenge rather than of hostility.

During the Civil War, the eagle was prominently displayed on northern regimental standards and was credited with having given extraordinary aid and comfort and inspiration among the Union ranks. One such mascot was dubbed old Abe and sworn in with a battalion from Wisconsin. The opposing Confederate general was heard to have admitted that he "would sooner capture that Yankee buzzard than a whole company."

Original carvings of the American eagle, ornamentations and reproductions, in various forms and attitudes, are eagerly sought after by collectors and antiquarians, and the "floating" supply is rapidly diminishing. It is well that so many patriots are anxious to preserve these replicas—rugged emblems of strength. Looking down upon us in solicitude from its lofty heights, this plumed sentinel seems to be ever reminding us of Gen. Washington's admonition: "Put only Americans on guard tonight."

> He clasps the crag with crooked hands;
> Close to the sun in lovely lands,
> Ring'd with the azure world, he stands,
> The wrinkled sea beneath him crawls;
> He watches from his mountain walls,
> And like a thunderbolt he falls.
>
> ALFRED LORD TENNYSON (1809-1892)

THE NATIONAL WONDERLANDS

How fortunate we are as Americans in the abundance of our national heritage, and especially our marvelous national parks, in which more and more millions find keen enjoyment each succeeding year. There are now twenty-nine of them, so located that one of perhaps several are readily accessible to all who ever take to the open road and go in search of adventure. Because of their careful selection, they run the whole range and are like samples of the original America. Some are very primitive areas, with the same strong appeal that the desert and wilderness have for many; while others are scenic, or have unmatched features equally worthy of being seen, investigated, absorbed. They exist for the diversion, instruction, and pleasure of all of us.

NELSON BEECHER KEYES, *America's National Parks;*
Doubleday, 1957.

Americans fortunately, possess a chronic wanderlust, a happy and beneficent curiosity to see and enjoy the priceless natural heritage which is theirs. Having earned the welcome solace of leisure, we are learning how to use it, enlarging the unprecedented incidence of people on the move, a mass mobility wherein we will all be guests of nature, which keeps offering us always something new to dwell upon— vistas and landscapes and scenic splendor and the satisfying sound of silence, a rare spiritual enrichment.

"America is a country of extremes," writes Archibald MacLeish. "The Republic is a symbol of union because it is also a symbol of differences, and it will endure not because its deserts and seacoasts and forests and bayous and dead volcanoes are of one mind but because they are of several minds and are nevertheless together. It is where the sand and the marsh and the rock and the grass and the great trees and the eternal wind compose the frontiers that there is greatness."

The system of National Parks was established by Congress forty-one years ago—the first such country in the world to set up such a bureau of land administration for public use and enjoyment. It has jurisdiction over 182 parks, monuments, historic sites, scenic and recreation areas, to which some 700,000,000 visits have been recorded. In August every year, Founders Day is celebrated with nation-wide observances; there are also Campfire Days, with local gatherings of park employees, friends, and visitors.

Our National Parks and dedicated sanctuaries are attracting visitors in ever-increasing numbers: a mere 380,000 in 1916, more than 20,000,000 in 1941, some 60,000,000 in 1957, with an estimated annual influx of 80,000,000 ten years hence. Accommodations and other tourist facilities are being constantly augmented, with additional camping sites, parking and picnic areas, as well as communication systems provided to increase the enjoyment of our irreplaceable national wonderlands. More than 200,000,000 acres of land are held and protected by the United States for its citizens within the boundaries of the system of National Parks and the national forests. No other nation in the world has set aside so great an area for the enjoyment and recreation of its people and for the conservation and development of its natural resources.

These permanent reservations known as public lands are owned by the people of the United States and are managed by the Federal Government under the jurisdiction of the National Park Service, a bureau of the Department of the Interior, with regional offices in Philadelphia, Richmond, St. Louis, Omaha, Santa Fe, San Francisco, where full information, regulations, and descriptive literature are readily available. Twenty-nine in number, these hallowed temples, which were not built with human hands and have been bequeathed to us as a sacred trust, are scattered all across the land: Acadia, the granite mountain of Maine; the Grand Canyon of Arizona and the Grand Teton peaks in Wyoming; the Great Smokies embracing the border between North Carolina and Tennessee; Mount Rainier in the state of Washington; Sequoia and Shenandoah, Yosemite and Yellowstone—"nature's greatest variety show." The newest addition to the chain of outdoor sanctuaries is the Virgin Islands National Park, which will preserve what is said to be one of the really unsullied beauty spots left anywhere in the world. On the Island of St. John in the Caribbean, acquired by the United States along with St. Croix and St. Thomas from Denmark, one-half of the ten thousand acres of lush forest has been donated by Laurence S. Rockefeller, who will restore the island's old plantations, which once enjoyed a thriving cultivation of sugar cane and tropical fruits. The natives—there are fewer than a thousand on the island—lead a tranquil, unhurried, primitive life among the dense growth of exotic flowers, shrubs, and useful plants.

Also maintained in thirty-nine states are one hundred and fifty national forests—our last remaining primitive wilderness—ranging in extent from one million to three million acres each. At Olympic National Forest in the state of Washington, predatory black bears are said to outnumber the human population 100 to 1 and may be hunted all year round by any means available. And not to be overlooked are the supplementary attractions of thirty-six National Nature Monuments, of which might be mentioned as most noteworthy Craters of the Moon, Dinosaur, Natural Bridges, the Petrified Forest, the Pinnacles, Shoshone Cavern. Seeing America first is the great adventure in recreation, meditation, and privileged citizenship.

> The national forests are the basis of our national conservation policy; they have been ever since Theodore Roosevelt took his great and decisive action fifty-one years ago. Because the public wealth they contain is so tempting to human and corporate greed, the war which conservation has to fight in defense of them never ends.
>
> They would cease to be in danger if the public took time to become better acquainted with its own possessions. No education could be pleasanter. Most people in the United States live within a few hours' drive of a national forest; no one lives more than a day's drive from one.
>
> Consider the probable population of the United States fifty or a hundred years from now. Consider the rapidity with which cities extend farther into the countryside and our industrial culture eats away our unspoiled country. Most of the remaining American wilderness that is not in the national parks is in the national forests, and all of it must be preserved. We originated as a wilderness people, our roots go back to the wilderness, and we must always have access to the physical and spiritual experiences that only the wilderness provides. And there is no bringing it back to its primitive condition once it has been changed.
>
> BERNARD DE VOTO, in *Your National Forests*

"UNCOMMON VALOR WAS A COMMON VIRTUE"

Soldiers, what I have to offer you is fatigue, danger, struggle and death; the chill of the cold night in the free air, and heat under the burning sun; forced marches, hazardous watchposts, and the continual struggle with the bayonet against batteries. Those who love freedom and their country may follow me.

GARIBALDI, to his Roman soldiers

The year 1776 saw the founding of the United States Marine Corps as a small detachment of "sea soldiers." In their long and honorable history, this contingent of fighting men, its strength since augmented to some 225,000 officers and men, has participated in the government action in every major war and insurrection in which the United States has been engaged. Accepting every challenge, asking no quarter and giving none, theirs is a heritage studded with gallant exploits and conspicuous valor.

At their fighting best, when the odds were against them, there has been a quality about the Marines which has commanded admiration wherever the action was joined—"from the halls of Montezuma," as the familiar hymn goes, "to the shores of Tripoli," epitomizing the far-flung services rendered by the Corps. The nation has become accustomed to taking a deep sense of assurance whenever the word was flashed: "The Marines have landed; the situation is in hand."

Never a summer soldier nor a sunshine patriot, the Marine prides himself on being always eager for a challenge —no matter how hazardous. Drenched in tradition, loyal to death, cocky and tough and proud, the Marines have a typical jingle:

> If the Army and the Navy
> Ever look on Heaven's scene,
> They will find the streets are guarded
> By United States Marines.

The late John Philip Sousa—the March King—was made bandmaster of the Marines when he began his career as a conductor, and his "Semper Fidelis" promptly became the keynote of the Corps.

In tribute to the voluntary six-man detachment—five Marines and a sailor—of whom only three survived the hazardous exploit of raising the Stars and Stripes atop Mount Suribachi on bloody Iwo Jima, an heroic bronze has been unveiled on a height along the Potomac near the Arlington National Cemetery. Graphically depicting one of the great moments in American history and executed by the sculptor Felix de Weldon, the statue, with its familiar straining figures five times life size, stands also as a stirring symbol of the gallant history of the Corps, and a memorial to all the Marines who have given their lives in the service of the country.

"For nearly two centuries," said Robert B. Anderson, Deputy Secretary of Defense, at the dedication, "the Marines have been engaged in building their own monument, not to temporal stone or bronze, but in the timeless realm of the human spirit. These figures represent man's highest hopes and greatest expectation, the sublime notion of his own ultimate capacity, under God, to work out his own salvation, both here and in the Kingdom to come."

The mountain fortress where a detachment of Japanese elected to dig in and die almost to the last man in its defense was the highest point on Iwo Jima. So bloody was the conflict that the Marines referred to it as "Mount Plasma." Despite its bombardment by American ships offshore, the enemy kept up an incessant rain of death upon the attacking troops on the beaches. "In this engagement," remarked Lt. Tittman, chaplain aboard the transport *Fayette,* "there were no rear areas. Everyone was under fire at all times." The casualties—Navy and Marines—exceeded 22,000 men; the Japanese counted more than 20,000 dead; the assault has been recorded as the fiercest landing fight the world had ever seen. Lying midway between Guam and Japan, Iwo is less than five miles long, but "never did so little mean so much to so many," for unless the island were taken, bombing raids of the American superforts would have been greatly curtailed by reduced range and effectiveness.

"It was," in the words of Winston Churchill, a "sacrifice for the causes by which the life and strength of mankind is refreshed. The United States has shown itself more worthy of trust and honor than any government of men or association of nations that has ever reached pre-eminence."

Inscribed on the base of the memorial is the benediction of Fleet Admiral Chester W. Nimitz—a tribute which might well apply to the entire Corps: "Uncommon Valor Was a Common Virtue."

The heroic exploit here commemorated is in a very real sense a glorification of youth. For in any "breakthrough" to new high ground, youth must spearhead the "bulge." And in youth's bright lexicon will be found few finer passages to ponder than the exhortation spoken by General of the Army Douglas MacArthur upon the occasion of the celebration of his seventy-fifth birthday:

Youth, as the poet has said, is not entirely a time of life—
it is a state of mind. It is not wholly a matter of ripe
cheeks, red lips, or supple knees. It is a temper of the
will, a quality of the imagination, a vigor of the emotions, a freshness of the deep springs of life. It means a
temperamental predominance of courage over timidity,
of an appetite for adventure over love of ease. Whatever
your years, there is in every being's heart the love of
wonder, the undaunted challenge of events, the joy and
the game of life. You are as young as your faith, as old
as your doubt; as young as your self-confidence, as old as
your fear; as young as your hope, as old as your despair.
In the central place of every heart there is a recording
chamber; so long as it receives messages of beauty, hope,
cheer and courage, so long are you young. When the wires
are all down and your heart is covered with the snows
of pessimism and the ice of cynicism, then and then
only, are you grown old.

THE RIGHT OF EXPRESSION

Without freedom of thought there can be no such thing as wisdom, and no such thing as public liberty without freedom of speech, which is the right of every man, as far as by it he does not hurt or control the right of another; and this is the only check it ought to suffer and the only bounds it ought to know. . . . Whoever would overthrow the liberty of a nation must begin by subduing the freedom of speech: a thing terrible to public traitors.

BENJAMIN FRANKLIN

Were it left for me to decide whether we should have a government without newspapers or newspapers without a government, I should not hesitate for a moment to prefer the latter. Where the press is free, and every man allowed to read, all is safe.

THOMAS JEFFERSON

At the corner of Wall and Nassau streets in New York City, on the historic site of Federal Hall, with its heroic statue of Washington taking the oath of office as first President in 1789, the John Peter Zenger Memorial commemorating the youthful pamphleteer's successful battle for a free press in America has been opened to the public as a national shrine—a fitting tribute to the immigrant German boy who courageously fought off the encroachments of the Crown upon what he conceived to be his right of expression. Some five hundred American newspapers and publishers contributed to the memorial, which includes dioramas and rare documents.

Arriving in the United States in 1710 and starting to work as a printer's apprentice, John Peter Zenger published the first issue of his New York *Weekly Journal* in 1733. It was a political organ founded by a group of New York citizens who opposed the policies and restrictions imposed by Colonial Governor William Cosby, who saw fit to condemn as "seditious reflections" the contents of the newspaper, causing the arrest of Zenger for libel, and, without a hearing, trial, or counsel, ordered him sentenced to prison.

While held in solitary confinement for almost a year, Zenger contrived, with the able assistance of his wife Anna, to have the *Journal* make its regular appearance. Although a reward was posted by the Governor for the apprehension of the author of the "offending" articles, the identity was never disclosed; but the conjecture was that they were written by Zenger's wife, a woman of unusual wit and talent.

As the time set for his trial finally approached, by great good fortune and to the consternation of the counselors of the Crown, Zenger obtained as his advocate the eminent lawyer, Andrew Hamilton, who came from Philadelphia to plead the cause, refusing to accept a fee of any kind for his services. His commanding presence, convincing argument, and simple eloquence so impressed the jury that a unanimous verdict of not guilty was promptly returned.

Mr. Hamilton's summation made it abundantly clear that a free press is an essential requisite if men are to be free:

I shall not myself live to see it, and many of you may not, but the time will come when, with fervent thankfulness, the people of this land will offer their prayers for all the freedoms that will be vouchsafed by this first and most important freedom for which John Peter Zenger dared to stand. The right of the people to worship according to their consciences cannot endure unless there is a free press to defend that freedom; the right of the people to assemble peaceably to demand redress of their wrongs cannot endure unless there is a free press to defend that right. You good people of New York have just witnessed the most important incident that may ever occur in the entire history of your city: you have seen freedom of the press established. I am humbly grateful that Mr. Zenger invited me to defend him here; and I would like also to pay my deep respects to his wife, who, during his imprisonment, carried on his work, and became the first woman newspaper publisher and editor—the Mother of Freedom.

Thus this obscure immigrant, with unflagging courage and constant vigilance, became the instrument and symbol of the struggle for a free press in the United States, his case establishing the first significant victory of the right of expression unshackled by arrogant censorship on the part of a biased judiciary. "The newspaper," wrote Samuel Bowles, founder of the Springfield *Republican*, "is the medium of thought and opinion, the circulating lifeblood of the human mind. It is the great enemy of tyrants, the right arm of liberty, and is destined, more than any other agency, to melt and mold the jarring and contending nations of the world into one great brotherhood, which, through the long centuries, has been the ideal of the Christian and the philanthropist."

These are the times that try men's souls. The summer soldier and the sunshine patriot will, in this crisis, shrink

from the service of their country; but he that stands it
now, deserves the love and thanks of men and women.
Tyranny, like hell, is not easily conquered, yet we have
this consolation with us, that the harder the conflict the
more glorious the triumph. . . . We fight not to enslave
but to set a country free, and to make room upon the
earth for honest men to live in.

THOMAS PAINE, *The Crisis* (1776)

UP FROM SLAVERY

I pity the man, black or white, who has never experienced the joy and satisfaction that come to a person by reason of an effort to assist in making someone else more useful and more happy. I have never sought or cared for what the world calls fame, having looked upon it as something to be used in accomplishing good.

PRESIDENT McKINLEY, at the Tuskegee Institute, 1898.

Born in 1856 of a family of slaves on a plantation in Franklin County, Virginia, Booker Taliaferro Washington, fired by a consuming zeal for learning and helpfulness, overcame the handicaps of a youth of hardship, poverty, and illiteracy, to become the foremost champion of the Negro race in the United States. Toiling long days in the coal fields and salt mines, going for long periods with scant food and clothing, often making his bed under a sidewalk, he permitted neither his lack of education, ostracism and often oppression of his race, nor any ordeal that confronted him to deter him from his high resolve.

Coming into the world without a name—the surname "Washington" was of his own choosing—never knowing the exact date of his birth, penniless, he presented himself at the age of sixteen, for admission to the Hampton Institute. Studious and always eager to perform the humblest tasks, he soon was promoted to the teaching staff. Here he insisted that his pupils appreciate the dignity and value of labor, that they keep their minds and bodies clean, respect their neighbors, and put their learning to practical use.

The Tuskegee Institute in Alabama stands as his greatest challenge and his living monument: a school for the practical training of Negroes in trades and professions. In 1881, the state had voted a sum for salaries, but the task remained for Booker Washington to build the physical plant, supervise the curriculum, and otherwise make Tuskegee a refuge and an opportunity in which his brothers and sisters might take pride and inspiration. He was a forthright evangelist for the cause he so ardently believed in, with a rare gift for oratory, a lively sense of humor, and unaffected common sense, attributes which stood him in good stead in his quest for contributions; there were very few, regardless of circumstance or prejudice, who would turn a deaf ear to his entreaties.

At his death in 1915, Tuskegee had a hundred buildings, a faculty of more than two hundred, a student body of some fifteen hundred, and an endowment fund of more than two million dollars. He was respected at home and abroad as a great educator and true philanthropist. He was sought after as a public speaker in the higher echelons of education; what he was accomplishing in humanitarianism, good citizenship, and popular enlightment was receiving world-wide recognition; the friend and associate of presidents and scholars, he had become one of the Western world's best known personalities. In 1940, his was the first portrait of an American Negro to appear on a United States postage stamp. "No man," he was wont to declare, "regardless of color, shall ever drag me so low as to make me hate him."

He was honored in 1945 by a place among the elect for outstanding accomplishments in the Hall of Fame at New York University; he was the first Negro to address a representative assemblage in the South, at the Atlanta Cotton Exposition; and in 1896 Harvard University gave him an honorary M.A. degree—the first time a New England college had ever conferred such a distinction on a member of the Negro race. His warmly greeted acceptance speech, made in the shadows of the splendor of Beacon Street, in striking contrast with his early environment in the Louisiana sugar bottoms and the Alabama cotton fields, bristled with his philosophy and ideals:

"In the economy of God there is but one standard by which an individual can succeed, there is but one for a race. This country demands that every race shall measure itself by the American standard. During the next half-century and more, my race must continue passing through the severe American crucible. We are to be tested in our patience, our forbearance, our perseverance, our power to endure wrong, to withstand temptations, to economize, to acquire and use skills; in our ability to compete, to succeed in commerce, to disregard the superficial for the real, the appearance for the substance; to be great and yet small, learned and yet simple, high and yet the servant of all."

And there was recently dedicated a National Monument near Joplin, Missouri, in tribute to another Negro who was to rise from slavery to eminence in the field of science— George Washington Carver, "the wizard of Tuskegee" (1864-1943). His research and successful application in botany and agriculture brought him wide recognition; he was made a fellow in the Royal Society of Arts in London, and received the Spingarn Medal for distinguished contributions in the study of plant life and crop propagation.

That man is a success who has lived well, laughed often, and loved much; who leaves the world better than he found it—whether by an improved poppy, a perfect

poem, or a rescued soul; who never lacked appreciation
of earth's beauty or failed to express it; who looked for
the best in others and gave the best he had. His memory
is a benediction.

ROBERT LOUIS STEVENSON

In a world that rolls on the brink of disaster it is easy
to say that the Negro should subordinate his fate to that
of his country and democracy. But there are no separate
fates. Negroes are Americans: they are fused into the
country's hillsides by the sweat of generations, by ages
of toil and bloodshed. The destiny of the American
Negro is also the destiny of America and democracy.
To protect its own permanent fate, freedom must cease
to be a sometimey, color-conscious thing.

CARL T. ROWAN, *South of Freedom;*
Alfred A. Knopf, 1952.

LITTLE RED SCHOOLHOUSES

The sheet-anchor of the Ship of State is the common school. Teach, first and last, Americanism. Let no youth leave the school without being thoroughly grounded in the history, the principles, and the incalculable blessings of American liberty. Let the boys be trained soldiers of constitutional freedom, the girls the intelligent lovers of freemen.

CHAUNCEY M. DEPEW

Though goodness without knowledge is weak and feeble; yet knowledge without goodness is dangerous; both united form the noblest character and lay the surest foundation of usefulness to mankind.

JOHN PHILLIPS, founder of Phillips Exeter Academy

The single-room Quasset School at Woodstock, Connecticut, opened in 1728 and in use until 1944, has been dedicated a national shrine and restored to its colonial appearance through the efforts of Mr. and Mrs. Albert H. Williams. Mrs. Williams taught there fifty years ago. Public-spirited citizens thus snatched the little red schoolhouse, erected two centuries ago, from the maw of the bulldozer. About thirty or forty fourth- and fifth-graders study their three R's around its ancient blackboard, which still bears familiar legends and time-honored problems. The pot-bellied stove is in its accustomed place; the old desk of the schoolmaster; the lunch pails, the water bucket and dipper; the high stool and dunce-cap; the slippery-elm switch stands in the corner, an "alert" to any nonconforming rebels.

A message received from President Eisenhower read: "This school should be the occasion for a rededication to the idea that an educated citizenry is a primary requisite for our own form of government. Under this principle the cause of good education must have the ardent and unremitting support of every citizen."

At Richmond Town—the old capital of Staten Island—a ten-cent ferry ride from Manhattan, another little red schoolhouse still stands, said to be one of the country's earliest elementary schools, dating from 1696. In Watertown, Wisconsin, there is a memorial to the first kindergarten in America, founded a hundred years ago by one Frederick Froebel, an intellectual refugee from an unsuccessful revolution in Germany. Supplementing these shrines commemorating our free-school system—one of the cornerstones of Americanism—is the traveling exhibit called "Schoolroom Progress, U.S.A." This miniature representation, installed on two railway cars designed and donated by the Chesapeake and Ohio Railroad and the Henry Ford Museum, has been open for inspection in several hundred cities across the country, showing the many advances made in public-school facilities and accommodations since the pioneer classrooms of the 1890's.

And one of the most noteworthy contributions to the public-school curriculum has been the decision of Congress to insert the words *under God* in the pledge of allegiance to the flag. This is of great significance to the millions of boys and girls now attending school, who will daily proclaim the dedication of our nation and our people to the protection of the Almighty, to our country's true meaning, and to a renewed faith in America's heritage and future: "Our children are born to higher destinies than their fathers; they will be actors in a far advanced period. Let their minds be formed, their hearts prepared, and their characters moulded for the scenes and duties of a brighter day." (*Youth's Companion*, 1827.)

Americans want their schools to be the best in the world; but to make them so, we must contribute more money, devote more time and imagination and intelligence, and develop more respect for our educational processes and for the dedicated teachers who represent them. Education is no longer the intellectual privilege of the gifted few but, rather, the democratic right of all; the pity of it is that there are not nearly sufficient buildings and classrooms, recreational facilities, and competent, adequately paid teachers: "To teach our sons and daughters, by precept and example, the honor of serving such a country as America is work worthy of the finest manhood and womanhood; high in the firmament of human destiny are set the stars of faith in mankind, and unselfish courage and loyalty to the ideal" (Henry Van Dyke).

Of growing concern, too, is the deteriorating average of physical fitness of our boys and young men; the elementary schools are slow in taking cognizance of this or in adopting measures designed to correct the deficiency. Dr. William L. Hughes, former professor of physical education at Columbia University, is authority for the statement that the continuing mechanization of life in the United States is having such a softening effect upon our youth as to constitute a real danger to the country: not more than 10 to 15 per cent of the nation's school children are being trained under an adequate physical-education program; only about one hour a week of 112 waking hours is now being devoted to physical fitness, whereas the time should be at least five times as much. And Columbia's president, Dr. Grayson Kirk, has spread dismay among teen-agers by advocating shorter summer vacations: is it common sense, he asks, for the American people to

spend vast sums of money on their school plants, only to
have them hopelessly overcrowded in winter and standing
idle during the summer? A lengthened school year, he thinks,
would benefit especially a million or more youngsters who
are now able to attend elementary schools only half a
day.

But commencement day would still be the customary
fixture of the school year, with its precepts and platitudes
and prescriptions for the good life issuing from principals
and pundits and pontifices, not forgetting the oft-expressed
nostalgia:

> And ye who will fill the places we once filled,
> And follow in the furrows that we tilled,
> Young men, whose generous hearts are beating high;
> We who are old, and about to die,
> Salute you; hail you; take your hands in ours
> And crown you with our welcome as with flowers!

In a lighter vein, the student body of the Lake Forest
(Illinois) Academy must have had a good chuckle from a
passage in the headmaster's talk as the school recently began
its one-hundredth year: "Just about seventeen years ago, a
new generation of locusts came into being, passing the dark
interval in an anonymous existence mostly underground
and unnoticed, to emerge not so long ago, stretch their un-
steady wings, proceed to eat all the available greenery, to
sing like mad far into the night, make a little love, crawl
far out on a limb, lay an egg or two, make the local head-
lines—and then disappear. What better and more timely
example could nature have furnished for the class of '56,
the year of the locust. All the story needs is the obvious
conclusion—and admonition: stay away from nature study,
don't sing too far into the night; don't get out on a limb;
and step on the next locust you see; the world you save
may be your own!"

Education does not mean teaching people what they do not know. It means teaching them to behave as they do not behave. It is not teaching the youth the shapes of letters and the tricks of numbers, and then leaving them to turn their arithmetic to roguery, and their literature to lust. It means, on the contrary, training them into the perfect exercise and kingly continent of their bodies and souls.

JOHN RUSKIN

A nation is strong or weak, it thrives or perishes, upon what it believes to be true. If our youth is rightly instructed in the faith of our fathers, in the traditions of our country, in the dignity of each individual, then our power will be stronger than any weapon of destruction that man can devise. My hope is that with advancing knowledge, toil will grow less exacting; that fear, hatred, pain, and tears may subside; that the regenerating sun of creative ability and religious devotion will refresh each morning the strength and progress of my country.

HERBERT HOOVER, at his homecoming at West Branch, Iowa

THE FUNDAMENTAL TRUTHS

. . . Now, Therefore, Be it Resolved, that the American Legion in national convention assembled at Washington, D.C., August 30—September 2, 1954, go on record as in favor of conducting a nationwide campaign to see that all state-supported institutions of higher learning require examination in U. S. history either to enter or to graduate; and, *Be it further Resolved,* That privately-endowed colleges and universities be requested to do likewise to the end that our American leadership will have knowledge of our history, traditions, ideals, personalities and economic and governmental systems.—*American Legion Convention Resolution*

It were well that the American people take seriously to heart the admonition of the American Legion to know America through American history—for without knowing her, we can neither love nor serve her nor keep abreast of her

150

destiny, never being fully aware of the social, physical, political, economic, intellectual, and spiritual forces which have
played upon her development for more than three centuries.
Indeed, it is a deplorable irony to contemplate that the widest experiment in public education in all history dismisses
its classes after having imparted only fragmentary knowledge
of the American people, American traditions, American institutions—allowing to pass virtually untapped the record of
the richest reservoir of human progress in the annals of
mankind.

All our historic shrines are eloquent and living and
visual testimony of America's greatness. Only through fa-
miliarity with the events, decisions, and personalities of the
past can we be made mindful of our freedoms and opportunities—and our obligations. "To fail our duties is to surrender our rights; no study, no tradition; no work, no salary;
no love of America, no protection from America. The
tragedy is that people who do not love God, generally do not
love America."

Nor can the nation be found lacking in facilities, facul-
ties, and literature for imparting the fundamental truths
about our forebears and ourselves. Scholars are emphatic
in their conviction that the most valuable writing issued in
this country during the past decade or two has been in the
fields of American history and biography—that as a people
we have only recently come to full realization of the richness
of our past and of the insufficiently explored areas of our
background, which are now being diligently mined for our
edification and example. Indeed, our schoolhouses in every
town and village, the ivied walls of our colleges and universities, can all become shrines of the living American past
if it were insisted that American history be accorded a more
dominant place in the curriculum.

A young university student won the eight-thousand-dollar
jackpot on a television quiz show recently introduced in
Italy. Her subject was American history. It is to be doubted
whether she would find much competition even from Ameri-

can students, until both our schools and our students evidence a greater interest in the history of their own country.

Consider such pertinent paragraphs as these from distinguished Americans:

The late Bernard De Voto in the Centennial issue of *Harper's* magazine: "And who were the American people? They were the product of the American continent, a new people in a new world. They were, for instance, the first people who were able to build a government and a society from the ground up—and on unencumbered ground; the first people in history who had ever had enough to eat; the first people whose society had the dynamics of political freedom and political security; and a common wealth so great that it made economic opportunity a birthright."

And Clarence Manion; "The need now is for rediscovery and renewed understanding of the true and tried principles of Americanism. While civilization exhausts itself in fruitless searches all over the world, it would be tragic indeed if this simple yet entirely effective formula for the complete peace and happiness of humanity is permitted to lie unheeded in the unturned pages of American history."

And yet competent authorities report that 67 per cent of our institutions of learning do not require a student to pass an examination in American history either to enter or to graduate; and whereas nearly all our leaders in government, in the professions, in business, commerce, and finance, have at least two years' college experience, the great majority of these leaders can boast of only fitful exposure to the record of our American heritage. Most American colleges and universities, to be sure, *offer* courses in United States history, but in the case only of a few is it a scholastic prerequisite. Thus the student leaves the cloister after having been steeped in ancient history and culture but with only a cursory, lukewarm reading in respect to his native land and its deep-seated meaning.

He will be unfamiliar with the roots from which America sprang, from its seedtime to its fullest flowering; he will have been made hardly aware of his country's beauty and splendor, its verities and opportunities, its trials and traditions. Nor will he have been encouraged to revive a neglected pride in its matchless qualities, or to become acquainted with the inspiring roster of the great men who made the nation great, or the significant events that marked its rise to acknowledged sovereignty. He will, later on, sorely miss the meaning of its institutions, the evolution of its religion, and its recreation, the obligations incumbent upon its citizens, the memorabilia re-creating the flavor and events of the American centuries. American history is the soul and sinew of the nation, a testament to which her sons may turn for courage and faith when they are faced with alien doctrines. What a pity, that so many of them must face the world knowing the Declaration, the Constitution, the Bill of Rights mostly by hearsay rather than by heart!

There are signs that adult Americans are more mindful of their national history than they used to be. To a greater extent we are revisiting the scenes of the past, our shrines and historic places. Our society seems to have more yearning for the past than nineteenth-century Americans had, and our generation more than any other has sought to recreate our relatively remote history. Historically, we have grown up. Far-sighted and generous individuals have perceived the need to conserve our historical as well as our natural resources, and our professional skill is proving fully equal to the challenge.
DUMAS MALONE, *Jefferson and His Times;*
Little, Brown & Co.

There is evidence that America is recovering the spirit that made it great. New words are appearing in our national vocabulary, words that have not been used in a political fashion in some time, words like "responsibility," "sacrifice," "work." This means a growing consciousness that freedom is preserved only by self-discipline. Science has not exempted us from the struggle for life: Freedom is something that has to be re-purchased every few decades by a nation. Liberty is no heirloom. It requires the daily bread of self-denial, the salt of law, and, above all, the backbone of acknowledging responsibility for our deeds.

BISHOP FULTON J. SHEEN

The time is opportune to reinform America of the inspiring story of our glorious democratic history of liberty, freedom, tolerance and justice. What is needed to revitalize the outlook of our youth is a total effort, beginning in elementary education and soundly bolstered in the home, to teach and preach the greatness of America, to make our history and our traditions live anew.

J. EDGAR HOOVER

"ONLY CHANGE IS CHANGELESS"

We live in the past by a knowledge of its history, and in the future by hope and anticipation. By ascending to an association with our ancestors; by contemplating their example and studying their character; by partaking of their sentiments and imbibing their spirit; by accompanying them in their toils; by sympathizing in their sufferings and rejoicing in their successes and their triumphs—we mingle our own existence with theirs and seem to belong to their age. We become their contemporaries, live their lives which they lived, endure what they endured, and partake in the rewards which they enjoyed.

DANIEL WEBSTER

Change is America's way of life; and as much as we are addicted to rapid alterations in our comings and goings, we still like to linger over our yesterdays, being aware that the past touches the present with light fingers: nostalgia is somehow always in the air. "America is a land of wonders," wrote De Tocqueville, the French historian, in 1836, "in which everything is in constant motion and every change seems to be an improvement. No natural boundary seems to be set to the efforts of man; and in his eyes what is not yet done is only what he has not yet attempted to do."

From the days of the deluge to the time of George Stephenson, the railroad builder, around 1820, water had afforded the easiest and cheapest form of transportation. In the United States, the towpath era, with its many miles of artificial channels, enjoyed a long head start over the conventional land carriers: a new link to the West, far better than the corduroy trails, had been found. A network of some five thousand miles of canals had been laid out at a cost of some two hundred million dollars, the money largely supplied by public subscription—one of the earliest risks of venture capital, not always with a happy ending. The Erie Canal, however, crossing the 350-mile width of New York State and joining Lake Erie with the Atlantic, gave commerce and industry a tremendous impetus. Disparagingly referred to as "Clinton's Ditch"—Gov. Clinton was the moving spirit of the project—the public was ultimately to give it the more dignified title of "the Grand Canal." Carl Carmer writes in *The American Story:* "Standards of living became higher as trade made more Americans prosperous; real estate and personal property rose in value along the canal; life became more leisurely and more cultural; the waterway made an impression on the life of the United States as a nation which has had a lasting and ennobling effect."

Presently the echo of the steam whistle was to sound against the banks of the Mohawk and the Erie, the Union and the Hennepin. Canals lacked the speed and flexibility to meet the demands of an ever-expanding continent; they were too narrow and too shallow, and they could not run uphill!

Before yielding to the unequal struggle, however, the canal gave America one of its most colorful, if not its most lucrative, periods of commercial traffic: gay packet parties on the decks of the *Yankee Spy,* the *Lady's Friend,* the *Sylvan Stream,* gliding down the placid waterways in the moonlight to the accompaniment of leisurely gossip, a quiet snooze, a minuet; or banjos strumming and passengers joining in some such rollicking refrain as "Storm on the Erie Canal"—an improbable disaster, but a jolly ballad that helped while away the hours of "the glory days," the Yankee challenge to the Mississippi showboats.

A well-loved segment of the American past came recently to life again when water was made to flow once more through the historic Delaware waterway between Easton and Bristol. Residents of this sixty-mile stretch of scenic beauty relived the long-past carefree days on the "big ditches," dressed in costumes of the period, the barges draped in red-white-and-blue bunting, the drag mules done up in their "Sunday best"—a gay and faithful pageant of the romantic inland waterways.

At Stony Brook, Long Island, the carriage house of the Suffolk Museum has been opened to the public, with a period collection of three hundred old carriages, carts, sleighs, and wagons: a hard-top buggy driven by Daniel Webster, President Buchanan's traveling coach, a Whitechapel cart, sulkies, a tally-ho, a cabriolet, a one-hoss shay. The exhibits also include a reproduction of a harness-maker's shop and a "smithy," equipped with original tools and paraphernalia. The assembly comprises a faithful, close-up view of the vehicles and trappings of the horse-and-buggy days.

Long destined to be "the city of travelers," New York annually throws open its hospitable gates to uncounted millions of visitors from far and near; and to whet their curiosity about antique vehicles and accouterments, the Museum of the City of New York on upper Fifth Avenue has established a comprehensive shrine of early locomotion. The exhibits depict also the styles in fashion and luggage as they kept pace with modes of travel over the years; the habits and clothing of the voyagers in and out of New York for two centuries are documented by costumed mannequins, ancient motor vehicles, woodcuts, paintings, sheet music and photographs, posters, advertisements, menus, and lists of nomenclature, as well as other pertinent memorabilia—a living chronicle of just about everything people did to get around from one place to another. Nor is ocean travel to and from the great port neglected: there is a replica of a stateroom of another period, with its double-decker bunks, hooked rug, and plush-covered settee—in contrast to the luxury of modern transatlantic accommodations, whether by sea or by air.

The ideal life is in our blood and never will be still. Sad will be the day for any man when he becomes contented with the thoughts he is thinking and the deeds he is doing—where there is not forever beating at the doors of his soul some great desire to do something larger, which he knows that he was meant and made to do.

BISHOP PHILLIPS BROOKS (1835-1893)

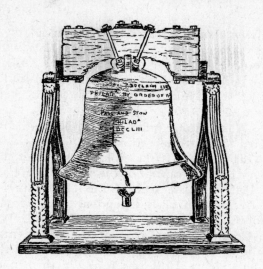

INDEPENDENCE MALL

Look back, therefore, with reverence, to the times of ancient virtue and renown; to the mighty purposes which your fathers had in view when they planted this land. Recall to your minds their labors, their toils, their perseverance and let their divine spirit animate you all in all your actions.

Look forward, also, then, to distant posterity. Figure to yourselves the millions and millions who are to spring from your loins, who may be born freemen or slaves, as Heaven shall now approve or reject your councils. Think, that on you may depend whether this great country, in ages hence, shall be filled and adorned with an enlightened people enjoying Liberty—or covered with a race of men more contemptible than the savages that roam the wilderness.

REV. WILLIAM SMITH (1775)

America will presently be welcoming another national shrine of paramount significance into its ever-lengthening roster of holy places, restored and preserved for our own and future generations. Independence National Historic Park is rapidly taking shape—Independence Mall, as it will be known—built around the central restoration of Independence Hall in Philadelphia, formerly the State House, dating from 1791, where "the United States was created" and where Washington, Jefferson, Franklin, and other patriots planned the birth of the nation.

From 1781 to 1783, Philadelphia was, under the Articles of Confederation, the capital of the United States, and Independence Hall was the seat of the Continental Congress when the Declaration of Independence was adopted. Here, also, a month after Lexington and Concord, Washington was made Commander-in-Chief of the continental armies; here was the first seat of the Supreme Court of the United States. Independence Hall was formally thrown open as a national museum in 1876, housing a rare collection of historic portraits of public men and of furniture, musical instuments, maps, manuscripts, coins, costumes, and weapons.

Here hangs the Liberty Bell, installed in 1752. "Proclaim Liberty throughout all the Land," its inscription reads, "unto all the inhabitants thereof"—a plea voiced in Leviticus thirty-five centuries ago. The clarion proved to be a brittle fabrication and had to be twice returned to its caster, Thomas Lister, of Whitechapel in London. The familiar crack running down its length occurred while a knell was tolling for Chief Justice John Marshall of the Supreme Court in 1835.

Redolent of the glory of the early days of the Republic, the spacious compound will contain within its limits other historic American shrines upon which millions of dollars and outstanding talents will have been spent in restoration of the colonial quadrangle—a stirring complement to the city of brotherly love, the "greene countrie towne," created by William Penn:

The Betsy Ross House, where, according to one of many

legends, the first Stars and Stripes was fashioned. Noted for her skill in sewing and needlework, Mrs. Ross was said to have been visited by Washington, Robert Morris, and an uncle, George Ross, and, after a discussion of the design was commissioned to execute the first national emblem.

Congress Hall, where Washington was inaugurated for his second term.

Carpenters' Hall, built in 1770 was the Guild Hall of the Carpenters' Company of Philadelphia, where the first Continental Congress met in 1774.

The Bank of the United States, said to be the oldest bank building in the country.

The Bishop White House, home of the Right Rev. William White, father of the Protestant Episcopal Church in America.

Beyond the confines of the Mall itself, the city of Philadelphia hopes to save and restore a portion at least of the 212-year-old Second Street Market. A fine example of colonial Georgian architecture, the building is the oldest standing market house in America and has been one of the city's most notable landmarks since the days of William Penn. Martha Washington and many prominent colonial dames regularly patronized the market's food stalls. Tucked in between factories and warehouses, Elfreth's Alley, the little cobblestone street between Front and Second streets, is believed to be the oldest street of homes in America. Its thirty-three dwellings, one dating from 1694, have all been occupied continuously for more than two centuries.

The tomb of Benjamin Franklin is in Christ Church Burial Grounds. In observance in 1956 of the two-hundred-and-fiftieth anniversary of the "universal man's" birth, the Post Office Department issued a three-cent stamp, reproducing the familiar painting "Franklin Taking Electricity From the Sky." The statesman, philosopher, and inventor spent his last twenty-five years in Philadelphia.

Washington wrote him shortly before his death: "If to be venerated for benevolence, if to be admired for talents, if to be esteemed for patriotism, if to be beloved for philanthropy can gratify the human mind, you must have the pleasing consolation to know that you have not lived in vain."

And Thomas Jefferson, writing eight years after Franklin's death, proclaimed him "the greatest man and ornament of the age and country in which he lived."

In more recent times, Joseph Medill, founding editor of the Chicago *Tribune,* bore witness to his greatness: "Since history has recorded human actions and deeds, who has performed more beneficial work for mankind? Who has added more to the stock of human knowledge than Franklin? Who has done more for human liberty or for the sons of toil, in rendering the lives of the common people happier or their lot more endurable, than Benjamin Franklin?"

Every American citizen is a sovereign, whether he chooses to exercise his sovereignty or not. The question is whether we shall be good or bad sovereigns, alert or apathetic ones, intelligent or stupid ones. Many Americans, through sheer indifference or incapacity, have abdicated their kingship. We have set up a representative government, and then all too often have failed to indicate in what way we wish to be represented. In 1776, we needed the consent of the governed; today we need *direction from the governed.*

THOMAS A. BAILEY, *The Man in the Street;*
Macmillan, 1948.

"I believe in one God, the creator of the universe; that He governs it by His Providence; that He ought to be worshipped; that the most acceptable service we render to Him is doing good to His other children. That the soul of man is immortal, and will be treated with justice in another life respecting its conduct in this. These I take to be the fundamental points in all sound religion."

BENJAMIN FRANKLIN

OLD NASSAU

Education in America is becoming increasingly characterized by technical considerations. The humanities have practically no place as compared with a French *lycee* or an English public school. Secondary education is carried out in the high school, which gives to all pupils, without selection, an excellent practical education with only a scanty academic background. Real culture is to be found only in the universities, but classical education is found only as a kind of accessory. . . . It is clear that the conditions under which a spirit of humanist culture is formed are very different from those which require the training of a worker to be efficient in the realm of collective action, whether one is considering industry, surgery, or social work. The specialist, who is well trained in his specialty, therefore becomes a necessity, and he must be given technical training, not general culture.

ANDRE SIEGFRIED, *America at Mid-Century;*
Harcourt, Brace and Co., 1955.

Built in 1756 from designs by Robert Smith of Scotland, Princeton University's Nassau Hall—affectionately known for two centuries as "Old Nassau"—is both one of our earliest academic landmarks and an historic shrine. For fifty years it was the college's only building, providing classrooms, chapel, dormitory, library, and dining rooms under its roof. Between 1746 and 1800 the largest graduating class numbered only thirty-seven students. In the Revolution, Nassau Hall, named in honor of William III of Orange and Nassau, the popular King of England, served as a barracks and as a hospital for Washington's forces and in 1783 as the United States Capitol. It was badly battered by gunfire during the battle of Princeton in 1777. It is being maintained as a general utility building, housing the administrative offices and made available for various other gatherings.

In commemoration of its bicentenary in 1956, the Post Office Department reproduced a front elevation of Princeton's first structure on its three-cent stamp.

"Postage stamps," Postmaster-General Summerfield has observed, "portray the ideals and aspirations of men and women of nations—the traditions, the progress, the geographic glories. They show in miniature its famous citizens, the great events of its history, its industries, its natural wonders. They disseminate ideas, and their study is a rewarding cultural hobby."

Following hard upon the bicentenary of Nassau Hall, the university elected as its sixteenth president Dr. Robert Francis Goheen, classicist, to succeed Dr. Harold Willis Dodds, retired. A member of the class of 1940, Dr. Goheen at the age of thirty-seven has become Princeton's third-youngest president. Only Aaron Burr, Sr., who took the chair in 1748 at the age of thirty-two, and Samuel Davies, inducted in 1759 at thirty-six, were younger.

Education is a big and vital business in America. In public and private funds we spend more than two billion dollars a year to maintain our thirteen hundred colleges, universities, teachers' colleges, professional and technical schools—

qualified to grant degrees in higher education—with an enrollment of some two and a half million young people, or about one boy and girl out of every six between the ages of eighteen and twenty-one. All the other nations of the world together cannot muster as many institutions of higher learning.

The anniversary celebration was the occasion for serious discussion of the form and direction of today's intellectual development. Supreme Court Justice John Marshall Harlan urged that Princeton continue to stress liberal education in "this complex and specific age": "We must take care that the place of liberal education in our scheme of things is not neglected. A purely scientific world is bound to be an unbalanced world, for science can but contribute to its material needs. It is also bound to be a dangerous world, for in the hands of untutored men, the revelations of science may yet be turned against society to its own destruction."

It may be timely to compare Justice Harlan's conclusions with those from the "prophetic soul" of Henry Adams expressed in a letter to his brother Charles, an officer in the Union Army in 1862, when the wooden ship began to see the handwriting on the wall: "I tell you these are great times. Man has mounted science, and is now run away with. I firmly believe that before many centuries more, science will be the master of man. The engines he will have invented will be beyond his strength to control. Some day science may have the existence of mankind in its power, and the human race commit suicide by blowing up the world. Not only shall we be able to cruise in space, but I see no reason why some future generation wouldn't give it another rotary motion so that every zone would receive in turn its due portion of heat and light." (Quoted by Allan Nevins in a review of *Henry Adams* by Elizabeth Stevenson, *American Heritage,* December, 1955.)

Or to weigh the testimony of the president of Yale University, A. Whitney Griswold (*Essays on Education,* Yale University Press) :

How may we Americans know ourselves so that we may know our weakness as well as our strength; so that we may understand the relationship between our cultural responsibilities and the political and military objectives to which we are committed; so that we may proclaim the virtues of American life in the universal language of humanity? The question leads straight to the liberal arts. These studies made their appearance in formal education in Greece, more than two thousand years ago. Plato and Aristotle both recognized their vital role in the education of the ideal citizen. There is much misunderstanding as to the meaning of the term "liberal arts." It means, and has meant from the beginning, the arts or studies becoming to a free man. Their purpose in our educational system was well stated by John Stuart Mill when he said it was to make "capable and cultivated human beings." . . . Men are men before they are lawyers or physicians or manufacturers; and if you make them capable and sensible men, they will make themselves capable and sensible lawyers or physicians.

PRINCE OF THE PLAINS

He was as real as Washington or Lincoln, Davy Crockett or Andrew Jackson. He fulfilled his own dreams and those of millions of admirers, fixing the image of the Wild West in the world's mind. He was legend as well as man; vain, but proud and generous, too. As the thousands streamed by his boyhood home in Kansas bound for California and the opening of a new country, he could no more resist joining the trek than a boy can resist following a parade; adventure and opportunity waited just beyond the horizon. Boy and man, saint and sinner, he symbolizes the picturesque heritage of the American frontier more forcefully today than he did at the many peaks of his earthly fame.

HENRY B. SELL & VICTOR WEYBRIGHT,
Buffalo Bill and the Wild West;
Oxford University Press, 1955.

William Frederick Cody—affectionately known round the world as Buffalo Bill—was born in Le Claire, Iowa, in

1846, and began at an early age a colorful career as rider for the Pony Express, army scout in skirmishes with the Indians, buffalo-hunter, and gentleman plainsman, the charm of his personality endearing him to young and old. But it was as a master showman—the presiding genius and bright particular star of Buffalo Bill's Wild West Show and Congress of Rough Riders of the World—that brought him his brightest fame at home and abroad and made him the darling of the era.

When he took the action-packed spectacle on the road, he thought to simplify the undertaking by announcing that "God will be my propertyman"; but as its popularity spread like a prairie fire he found himself with a staff of some five hundred performers, artists, and assistants: Indians, cowboys, Mexican *vaqueros,* broncos, buffalo, the Deadwood coach, and the peerless lady wingshot, Annie Oakley, who, during her seventeen years as heroine of the show, never— or hardly ever—missed her target. "The Prince of the Plains was right," said his biographers; "God *had* set the stage: the Wild West."

"Take the prairies and the Injuns and the horses and the buffalo and the old stagecoach and everything right to the people of the East," one of his cronies urged him; "that would be something they'd never seen before! That would be showing them the West."

Folks flocked to every performance, in whatever city, town, or hamlet it took place. The show toured Europe, amazed dignitaries and commoners alike with its tumultuous backdrop of the West. Buffalo Bill became the toast of crowned heads, potentates, and presidents. In Paris, in 1889, Rosa Bonheur painted his portrait, life-size, in full regalia on his white charger.

Col. Cody was devoted to the younger generation and was patron saint of the Boy Scouts of America. In talking to boys, he would tell them that if he were a boy again he would certainly join the Scouts. When his Wild West troupe was playing in Chicago near the World's Fair grounds,

Mayor Harrison had asked Fair officials to admit poor children of the city free on a special day. When his request was refused, the colonel forthwith announced that the show would not only admit them free but would also provide free transportation, free candy, and free ice cream, with the result that fifteen thousand delirious youngsters spent the most exciting afternoon of their lives.

The memorial to the great man of the plains is a typically American shrine at Cody, Wyoming. On a broad mesa between Rattlesnake and Cedar mountains stands a twelve-foot bronze statue by the sculptress Gertrude Vanderbilt Whitney, faithfully depicting the scout mounted on "Old Smoky" and scanning the ground for pony tracks of the Sioux. Nearby is the Buffalo Bill Museum, where visiting laymen and scholars will find a wealth of western memorabilia: guns, knives, uniforms, trappings, vehicles, harness, medals, trophies, thousands of letters, hundreds of the popular Buffalo Bill dime novels of thrills, adventure, heroism, and hairbreadth escapes, and a varied collection of authentic western paintings, prints, sculpture, and photography. And it must please his departed spirit that not too far distant, at Oklahoma City, a national Cowboy Hall of Fame has been dedicated in which seventeen neighboring states have joined to sponsor a million-dollar museum and memorial to riders of the range both past and present.

Some years ago, when the old Madison Square Garden in New York was witnessing the final performance of the Wild West show, it was announced that after the final act Col. Cody would like to say a last farewell to the American public. The riders backed their mounts against the dropcurtain portraying lively scenes of the West and the spotlight came full upon Buffalo Bill, still a commanding, courtly figure on his cream-colored charger, dressed in his familiar regalia—broad-brimmed Stetson hat, fringed buckskin jacket—his snow-white locks flowing in the breeze.

"In spite of all the things I may have done wrong," he began, "if I have succeeded in bringing to the youth of

America the plains, the cowboy, the Indian, the buffalo, the covered wagon, the mail coach; if, indeed, I have been successful in bringing the romance of America to the hearts of young America, I have not lived in vain."

Buffalo Bill died broken in purse but not in spirit at the age of seventy-one. He is buried atop Lookout Mountain in the Rockies, a short distance outside of Denver, far from his beloved Wyoming "foothills of heaven."

All the distortions of romance cannot alter the fact that the real story of the American people is a tale of high adventure. The record of events on our side of the ocean from 1492 to the present constitutes one of the most romantic stories in the history of mankind.

ARNOLD WHITRIDGE, *The American Enigma*

MAN OF THE PEOPLE

Each Easter time, the people of America take over their capital city. Parents bring their children down from the coves and valleys of the Blue Ridge to see the great national shrines. Teachers bring their students from across the plains to remind them what America means. They see what endures: not the villains and the twisters, not merely the clever and successful, but the true, the honorable and the beautiful. What constitutes the bulwark of our own liberty and independence? Here is Lincoln still saying to the children from the prairies:

"It is not our frowning battlements, our bristling sea coasts, our army and our navy. Our reliance is in the spirit which prized liberty as the heritage of all men, in all lands everywhere. Destroy the spirit, and you have planted the seeds of despotism at your own doors.

JAMES RESTON in the New York *Times*

And visitors will pause at the majestic Lincoln Memorial in Potomac Park to meditate upon the greatness of the man who rose from backwoods obscurity, untutored but resolute and self-reliant, to lead his country through its most momentous crisis. This impressive monument to a public servant of unswerving devotion, marked from humble birth for a higher destiny, is one of the most beautiful edifices in America, and one of the tallest ever erected in tribute to any man. Its exterior symbolizes the Union of the nation, its walls surrounded by thirty-six Doric columns of white marble, representing the states that existed at the time of Lincoln's death. The place of honor within the sanctuary is occupied by a colossal marble statue of the Civil War President, modeled by Daniel Chester French and facing the Washington Monument and the Capitol. Running off from the memorial is a reflecting pool 2,000 feet long, with a fountain of two hundred jets.

Lesser shrines, too, recall the life of the Great Emancipator—more dedicated places, perhaps, than have been set apart to honor the memory of any other American. Near Hodgenville, Kentucky, in the Abraham Lincoln National Park, there is a Greek-style memorial housing the crude one-room log cabin—dirt floor, a solitary window, a bed of corn husks and bearskins—reputedly the place of his birth, on February 12, 1809, on a worthless track of land called Sinking Spring Farm. One wonders, indeed, how the son of Tom and Nancy Lincoln could ever have survived infancy under conditions of such squalor and marginal means of existence. Near Lincoln City in Spencer County, Indiana, where the family moved after seven years of grubbing in the Kentucky hills, is the Lincoln State Park, with memorial buildings to Lincoln and his mother. Still in his early teens, he here began his self-education.

Said his cousin, Dennis Hanks: "I have never seen Abe without a book. He'd put a book inside his shirt and fill his pants pockets with corn dodgers an' go off to plow or hoe; when noon came he'd set under a tree an' read an' eat; an' at night he'd tilt a chair back by the chimbly an' read some more."

During the fourteen years of residence in Indiana, Lincoln got along by running a ferryboat across Pigeon Creek, working on the land as a hired hand, clearing woods, splitting rails, and running errands down the river to New Orleans.

At New Salem, Illinois, on the Sangamon River, where the family next settled, the State Park Restoration is a shrine to Lincoln's formative years. Here he conducted a general store, enlisted in the militia for the Black Hawk War in 1832, practiced surveying, became the town's postmaster, and lost election to the Illinois General Assembly, to which he was elected four years later. Here was the scene also of the romance of Lincoln's youth with the innkeeper's daughter, Ann Rutledge.

In Springfield stands the only home Lincoln ever owned, at the corner of Eighth and Jackson streets, where he brought his family in 1844 and where he was to engage in law and politics and become famous for his oratory and statesmanship in the widely publicized debates with the "little giant," Stephen A. Douglas, then Democratic senator from Illinois. In the parlor of his home there, Lincoln received the news of his nomination for the presidency.

Upon his election in 1861, he took leave of his fellow citizens with these prophetic words: "No one, not in my situation, can appreciate my feelings of sadness at this parting. To this place, and the kindness of these people, I owe everything. Here I have lived a quarter of a century, and have passed from a young to an old man. Here my children have been born, and one is buried. I now leave not knowing when, and whether ever, I may return, with a task before me greater than that which rested on Washington."

Lincoln is buried in the city's Oak Ridge Cemetery, where his tomb is a national shrine and the scene of pilgrimages the year round to pay homage to this man of the people, the hero of the common man. Beneath the tall spire of the monument are four groups of heroic bronzes representing the infantry, the cavalry, the Navy, and the artillery of the Union forces. Embossed in bronze over the entrance to the tomb are Lincoln's memorable words ". . . dedicated to the proposition that all men are created equal."

The small first-floor bedroom in the Peterson lodging house, across Tenth Street from Ford's Theater, where Lincoln lay through the night mortally wounded by an assassin's bullet, is maintained for posterity exactly as it was in the early morning of April 15, 1865, and where, as Lincoln's life ebbed away, Secretary Stanton spoke the memorable words: "Now he belongs to the ages." And as a final tribute, the heroic image has been hewn out of the granite face of Mount Rushmore in the Black Hills of South Dakota by Gutzon Borglum, in the valiant company of Washington, Jefferson, and Theodore Roosevelt.

In a single summer, a million people gaze spellbound at the colossal likeness. Were the busts full figures, each would measure 465 feet tall. "I wanted," said the sculptor, "somewhere in America a few feet of stone that would bear witness to the great things we have accomplished as a nation, placed so high it would not do to pull it down for lesser purposes, carved as close to heaven as we can."

With malice toward none, with charity for all, with firmness in the right as God gives us to see the right, let us strive on to finish the work we are in, to bind up the nation's wounds, to care for him who shall have borne the battle, and for his widow and his orphan, to do all which may achieve and cherish a just and lasting peace among ourselves and with all nations.

Lincoln's Second Inaugural Address, March 4, 1865

We have been the recipients of the choicest bounties of heaven. We have been preserved these many years in peace and prosperity. We have grown in numbers, wealth and power as no other nation has ever grown, but we have forgotten God. We have forgotten the gracious hands which have preserved us in peace, which have multiplied us and strengthened us, and we have vainly imagined in the deceitfulness of our hearts, that these things were produced by some superior wisdom and virtue of our own. Intoxicated with unbroken success we have become too self-sufficient to feel the necessity of redeeming and preserving grace, too proud to pray to the God that made us.

ABRAHAM LINCOLN

In this temple
As in the hearts of the people
For whom he served the Union
The memory of Abraham Lincoln
Is enshrined forever.

Inscription on the Lincoln statue in Washington

THE VOICE OF DEMOCRACY

From youth he felt himself marked for a great task. His life was as a landscape across which sunlight and clouds passed alternately; and the climax was a storm in which the gods themselves seemed locked in conflict. The man who passed through these vicissitudes, by his gifts and ardors calling up the whirlwind, was frail in health, reserved and lonely in disposition, an unshakeable spirit suffused with inner light, who went forth to meet the destiny awaiting him; aspiring, eager, as one in whom the dreams of youth live on to become mingled with the attainments of maturity.

AUGUST HECKSCHER, *The Politics of Woodrow Wilson;* Harper's, 1956.

Marking the one-hundredth anniversary of the birth of Thomas Woodrow Wilson, twenty-eighth President of the United States, three memorials honoring him, respectively, as a former head of Princeton University, Governor of the state of New Jersey, and Chief executive and world statesman are in progress or have been completed.

176

Wilson was born in Staunton, Virginia, on December 28, 1856, and his birthplace is being restored and has been dedicated as a national shrine. His permanent tomb has been erected in a memorial bay in the new Washington Cathedral nave now under construction, adjoining memorials to Robert E. Lee and Stonewall Jackson; he being the eighty-second person to be honored in the Hall of Fame at New York University, the twelfth President and the sixth college president to be so represented, a bronze bust has been installed in the statesmen's pavilion there.

Scholar and reformer, Woodrow Wilson—he had dropped his first name while a boy, as had Stephen Grover Cleveland before him—brought honor and integrity to each of the offices he occupied, adorning them with wisdom and a rare grace of expression. Dedicated to vital democratic principles, he attempted social reforms at Princeton calculated to hold open to all rather than to a favored few the rights and privileges and advantages of the University.

"The great voice of America," he wrote, "does not come from the seats of learning. It comes in a murmur from the hills and woods and farms and factories and the mills, gaining in volume until it comes to us from the homes of common men. The universities would make men forget their common origins, forget their universal sympathies, and join a class—and no class can ever serve America. I shall not be satisfied until America shall know that the men in the colleges are saturated with the same thought, the same sympathy, that pulses through the whole great body politic."

Called from the cloister at Princeton to the governor's office, he welcomed the opportunity of fighting a well-entrenched political machine, instituting a reform program which attracted national attention: "Politics ought not to be considered as a mere occasion for oratory, but as a branch of the national business. Who would say that this is not an exalted function? Who shall doubt or dispraise the title of leadership?"

During Wilson's two terms as President were enacted

the Federal Reserve Act, the Clayton Antitrust Act, a child-labor law, lower tariff schedules, and establishment of the Federal Trade Commission. Following World War I, his great dream of world peace rested with the Treaty of Versailles, which included the League of Nations Covenant; but a "vaulting ambition had o'erleapt itself," and he was dealt a crushing blow when the Senate failed to ratify.

From his prolific and profound prose, the following four brief passages have been selected for the wall tablets to be incorporated in the Washington Cathedral Memorial:

From his first inaugural address: "This is not a day of triumph; it is a day of dedication. Here muster, not the forces of party, but the forces of humanity. Men's hearts wait upon us; men's lives hang in the balance. Who shall live up to the great trust? Who dares fail to try?"

From the war message to Congress: "The right is more precious than peace, and we shall fight for the things which we have always carried nearest our hearts—for democracy, for the right of those who submit to authority to have a voice in their own government, for the rights and liberties of small nations."

Upon the submission of the peace treaty to the Senate: "The stage is set, the destiny is closed. It has come about by no plan of our conceiving, but by the hand of God, who led us into this way. We cannot turn back. We can only go forward, with lifted eyes and freshened spirit, to follow the vision."

From his last published words: "The sum of the whole matter is this, that our civilization cannot survive materially unless it be redeemed spiritually. It can be saved only by becoming permeated with the spirit of Christ and being made free and happy by the practices which spring out of that spirit."

Wilson's dictum that the United States was born to redress the tyrannies and uplift the backward peoples of the world lived on as the gospel of the Democratic party to justify intervention by Democratic administrations in foreign wars and now has become the doctrine of the internationalists dominating both parties.

ARTHUR SEARS HENNING, Chicago *Tribune*

His inflexibility was the tragic flaw in the character of a great and good man. It was to be Wilson's fate to face the greatest crisis in the nation's history since Abraham Lincoln did battle with the forces of slavery and secession. To him was granted a chance to change the course of world history. Like Lincoln he met the challenge with vision, courage, dedication, and determination; he failed because he lacked Lincoln's greatest virtue—humility.

JOHN A. GARRATY, in *American Heritage* Magazine

SAGAMORE HILL

I believe in honesty, sincerity and the square deal; in
making up one's mind what to do—and doing it—
I believe in fearing God and taking one's own part—
I believe in hitting the line hard when you are right—
I believe in speaking softly and carrying a big stick—
I believe in hard work and honest sport—
I believe in a sane mind in a sane body—
I believe we have room for but one soul—loyalty, and
that is loyalty to the American people.
My Creed, by Theodore Roosevelt

Another historic shrine has been added to the inspiring
roster of America's dedicated places that contribute so im-
portantly to the tone of the American scene and serve as
such a bracing tonic to our remembrance. Sagamore Hill,
at Oyster Bay, Long Island, has taken its rightful place
among the restorations of homes of former Presidents.

This well-loved retreat was built in 1884 by Theodore Roosevelt, the nation's twenty-sixth President, opposite whose name history has recorded a glittering succession of accomplishments perhaps unmatched by any public servant of modern times. Its familiar gables and spacious porches, specimens from the wilds, trophy rooms, and notable memorabilia have been faithfully preserved, as has been the spirit of the dwelling place. It was to this tranquil atmosphere and to the bosom of his family circle that this man of action, the "man on horseback," the "man with a big stick," the "Rough Rider," the "Bull Moose,"—the popular personification of the strenuous life throughout most of his sixty-one years—always wanted most to repair.

"At Sagamore Hill," he liked to say, "we love a great many things—birds and trees and books and all things beautiful and horses and rifles and children and work and the joy of life."

Despite our tensions, the United States remains a happy land, the land of good cheer, God's country. It produces the Optimists' Club, the Glad Books, the Boosters' Society, manuals on how to attain peace of mind, songs to the effect that though "I want to be happy, I can't be happy unless you're happy, too."

In the nineteenth century, statesmen were statesmen and took a statesman's stance, but beginning with Teddy Roosevelt's teeth, our presidents have radiated gladness—Taft's chuckle, Wilson's fondness for limericks, Harding's geniality, Coolidge's Yankee witticisms, F.D.R.'s smile, Harry Truman's grin. Parenthetically, one notes that the only vice-president aging voters remember as such, is the man who got off the wisecrack about the five-cent cigar.

HOWARD MUMFORD JONES, *The Pursuit of Happiness;*
Harvard University Press, 1953.

At the dedication ceremonies in 1953, President Eisenhower called for a "spontaneous tribute to one of the greatest Americans, who by his life built a monument to America." And a fellow townsman added this: "Today we talk of programs, of a broader outlook, of human rights, and the equality of man as if these things were something new. Yet half a century ago, this man we called 'Teddy' spoke for, preached for, and lived for those very ideals we now so fervently extoll." The plain people had an affection for him such as they had not lavished upon any other public man since Lincoln.

Physically frail in childhood, by sheer determination and long periods outdoors in the hills of North Dakota, he conquered his handicaps and came to be known as an "interesting combination of St. Paul and St. Vitus," so tireless was he in thought and execution, endowed with such superhuman energy. Of gentle birth and breeding, he remained a man of the people and the enemy of malefactors of great wealth. To recount his manifold interests and accomplishments is to cite an unmatched record of public service.

An unsuccessful candidate for mayor of New York City in 1886, he first entered public life as a civil-service commissioner, then as president of the Board of Police Commissioners. He was made Assistant Secretary of the Navy in 1897, and when war broke out with Spain the following year, he resigned, with Leonard Wood organized the Rough Riders, and as their colonel led the charge up San Juan Hill. Elected Governor of New York, he instigated far-reaching reforms against corruption and political bosses. Upon McKinley's death he became, at the age of forty-three, the youngest President in the history of the United States and was re-elected in 1904. His domestic policies were concerned chiefly with attacks on the spoils system, trust-busting, conservation of natural resources, railway-rate legislation; he instituted the Departments of Labor and of Commerce, the Pure Food and Drug Act, and employers'-liability laws.

In the wake of some erratic diplomacy, he obtained the right to build a canal across Panama and, for his successful intervention in the Russo-Japanese War in 1905, was awarded the Nobel Peace Prize. However, being out of sympathy with the policies of President Taft, who succeeded him, he split violently with the Republican Party and as nominee of the Progressives for President was defeated by Woodrow Wilson in 1912. He was a naturalist and a world traveler, and there followed his famous expedition into Brazil, where he explored "the River of Doubt," since named Rio Theodoro in his honor. He was refused his insistent request to form and command a division in World War I, in which his four sons served, one being killed and two wounded. He died at Sagamore Hill on January 6, 1919.

When you, Susie, who are now eight, are grown up and have children of your own, I believe that you will want to be the kind of mother that Mrs. Roosevelt was: loving, strong and understanding, ready always to listen and to laugh, keeping promises, bringing the heroes of poetry and history into your children's lives, waking the love of God in their hearts, and so shaping their minds and spirits that they may be capable of sustaining the privileges and responsibilities of freedom.

And when you, Mickey, who are seven, are grown up and have a family, I believe that you will want to be as tender, true and gay a father as Theodore Roosevelt; a playmate to your children, as young as they in a race or a roughhouse, yet always helping them to grow in strength, compassion and courage; expecting the best from them, yet never too hard on them when they fall short; summoning them ever to richer adventure, higher service, and yourself leading the way, fearing God and taking your own part.

HERMANN HAGEDORN, to his grandchildren, from
The Roosevelt Family of Sagamore Hill;
Macmillan, 1954.

The most complete and flawless success of Theodore Roosevelt's career was not as pater patriae but as pater familias. He was a supremely great family man because he worked at it as hard as he worked at anything in his life. The wisdom and grace of his letters to his children raised them to a level unsurpassed by any correspondence of that sort in the English language.

GERALD W. JOHNSON, *The Lunatic Fringe;*
Lippincott, 1957.

Our country calls not for the life of ease, but the life of strenuous endeavor. The twentieth century looms before us big with the fate of many nations. If we stand idly by, if we shrink from the hard contests where men must win at hazard of their lives and at the risk of all they hold dear, then the bolder and stronger peoples will pass us by and they will win for themselves the domination of the world. America is a demanding country. Simply because it offers us more than any other country offers its people, it expects more in return. We had to work for what we have and we shall have to work to keep it. We are face to face with our destiny and we must meet it with a high and resolute courage. For us is the life of action, of strenuous performance of duty; let us live in the harness, striving mightily; let us rather run the risk of wearing out, rather than of rusting out.

THEODORE ROOSEVELT

"THE LION AND THE FOX"

Franklin D. Roosevelt was himself passionately committed to democracy as a philosophy and as a way of life; and it was during his administration that the basic assumptions of democracy were challenged and required to justify themselves. It is sometimes submitted as a criticism of democracy that it does not lend itself readily to precise definition, or that it appears to change meaning from generation to generation. What this means is that democracy is as much an attitude of mind and inclination of heart as a particular body of beliefs or practices, and that it can adapt itself to historical change.

HENRY STEELE COMMAGER, *Living Ideas in America;*
Harper's, 1951.

In the years of a paralyzing depression during the 1930's and of a consuming World War in the 1940's, democracy in America faced the supreme test of survival under the direction and philosophy of President Roosevelt, who, disregarding pledges and precedence and tradition, asked for and received from the American people a mandate for leadership for four consecutive terms of office. With this audacious departure from usage, custom, and restriction, democracy under his aegis was to take on new interpretations, new meaning, new concepts of human needs; unfamiliar and often confusing guideposts were to appear along the nation's well-beaten and long-established line of march.

Master of rhetoric, lavish in the use of catchphrases— "economic royalists," "money-changers in the temple," "the only thing we have to fear is fear itself," "I say again, and again, and again, that your sons will not be sent abroad to fight foreign wars," the "welfare state," "pump-priming," "the nine old men"—Franklin Roosevelt had the facility for telling the people what they wanted to hear, even if on occasion the telling was done with tongue in cheek. For when he took office in 1933 the time was ripe for a new look at democracy: industry was prostrate; nine million were unemployed; banks throughout the land were closing their doors; manipulation and speculation—and peculation—had been rampant. The people, confronted with chaos, were on the threshold of despair.

"What gave the New Deal its distinction," wrote Donald H. Sheehan in *This Is My Country* (Wm. H. Wise & Co.), "was not so much the character of the changes as their bewildering quantity. If action was what the country demanded, Roosevelt certainly fulfilled its hopes during the famous 'Hundred Days' after his inauguration. The Government had shifted from defensive measures designed to minimize the depression to an active offensive to obliterate it. A bold willingness to strike out in new directions and proceed by trial and error had long been characteristic of American society; but so varied and radical were the experiments conceived and set in motion by the President's hand-picked 'brain trust' that they often conflicted with one another, producing confusion rather than progress."

By such improvisations and novel contrivances, if F.D.R. had changed the complexion of the American economy, he had, nonetheless, got it working again. His later immersion in world affairs was not to turn out so auspiciously. One of the most controversial and contradictory figures ever to appear on the American scene, he has left historians, of all political persuasions, in wide disagreement over his ultimate historical role. Certainly the final verdict will not be resolved in this generation.

The Franklin D. Roosevelt Memorial Library adjoins the family estate overlooking the Hudson River at Hyde Park. Some four hundred thousand dollars were raised by voluntary subscription and the shrine is administered by the National Archives under a joint resolution of Congress. More than a half million persons visit the premises annually, where there are preserved and made available for research an extensive collection of state papers, manuscripts, correspondence, records and historical material. In a rose garden nearby, a plain white marble headstone marks the grave of the thirty-second President. And at Warm Springs, Georgia, "The Little White House," a beneficial retreat for those afflicted with the ravages of polio, is a living reminder of the gallant battle he waged against the dread disease which left him a cripple at the age of thirty-nine. He died there, April 12, 1945, in his sixty-third year. Basil O'Connor, head of the Georgia Warm Springs Foundation, has announced a Polio Hall of Fame, with busts of seventeen persons prominently identified with the long battle against the disease, to be set in Founders Hall, the Foundation's new administration building.

Should you and I lose the sacred fire of liberty—and if we let it be smothered with doubt and fear—then we shall reject the destiny which Washington strove so valiantly to establish. In the face of great perils never before encountered, our strong purpose is to protect and to perpetuate the integrity of democracy. For this we must muster the spirit of America and the faith of America. We do not retreat. We are not content to stand still. As Americans we go forward, in the service of our country, by the will of God.

—*Roosevelt's Third Inaugural Address*

Since the beginning of our American history we have been engaged in change—a perpetual peaceful revolution. The world order which we seek is the cooperation of free countries, working together in a friendly, civilized society. This nation has placed its destiny in the hands and hearts of its millions of free men and women; and its faith in freedom under the guidance of God. In the future days which we seek to make secure, we look forward to a world founded upon these four essential human freedoms: freedom of speech and expression, freedom of every person to worship God in his own way, freedom from want, freedom from fear.

Roosevelt's Annual Message to Congress (1941)

Here is one-third of a nation ill-nourished, ill-clad, ill-housed—

Here are thousands upon thousands of men and women laboring for long hours in factories for inadequate pay—

Here are thousands upon thousands of children who should be at school, working in mines and mills—

Here are strikes more far-reaching than we have ever known, costing millions of dollars—

Here are spring floods threatening to roll again down our river valleys—

Here is the dust bowl beginning to blow again—

If we would keep faith with those who had faith in us, if we would make democracy succeed, I say we must act NOW!

Roosevelt's Address at a Democratic Victory Dinner
(1937)

SHRINES OF FREE ENTERPRISE—1

When the American consumer wants something he wants it quickly, and in huge quantities, and at low cost. It has been so since the country existed. First it was nails, to help meet the housing shortage that followed after the Revolution; then pins, which were so rare that the housewives used them as a form of barter, or "pin money"; then it was clocks, pots and pans, hats, clothing, soap, farm equipment, furniture; and by 1900, the rather more complicated "horseless carriage." But some inventive genius always stepped into the breach with a mass production formula to knock down costs and thus make available to the people essentials and comforts and luxuries.

Du Pont: The Autobiography of an American Enterprise; distributed by Scribner's

More and more business concerns in the United States are assembling their own museums by way of bringing home to the public the history and constant improvement of their products and methods of manufacture and distribution, promoting good will, and enhancing popular acceptance. Whereas before World War I there were probably not more than a dozen of these corporate exhibits open to the public, they have met with such high favor that today there must be several hundred of them.

An inventive turn of mind, an eager grasp of material things, have constantly brought new devices and designs to our doorsteps. We have had only to express a wish or even to feel the need of some helpful complement to our lives, and almost before another sun had set, some agile wizard will contrive a new satisfaction. The lesson of American invention is that Americans never turn away from bold undertakings, take no stock in the false assumption that there are no new frontiers to conquer, are always ready to accept a challenge.

History is anything but "bunk" at the Henry Ford Museum and Greenfield Village at Dearborn, Michigan, as the founder and patron saint of this earliest of American business shrines once chose to call it. For a reverence for the past permeates this vast exhibit of historically significant technological, educational, and artistic Americana. Because of its nominal admission charge, it has been called the "biggest bargain in nostalgia"; its priceless panorama of buildings, machinery, products, and inventions, tracing in actual working order the development of industrial and cultural life in the United States.

The more than one hundred reconstructed shops and factories and mills, as well as a number of famous early-American homes of historic interest, scattered over two hundred sprawling acres giving onto the Village Green, faithfully depict the arts and crafts, the home life, and the means of locomotion, the tools, and the utensils of a hundred years ago—all activated, to import a working knowledge of every function.

Dedicated to Ford's intimate friend, Thomas A. Edison,

the Edison Institute houses the latter's Menlo Park laboratory and its early contrivances, the birthplace of the incandescent light and other startling inventions. A novel se-
quence shows the whole history of illumination, from Nero
to neon. The Hall of Mechanical Arts exhibits 175 antique
autos of every make, style, and vintage, all restored to their
best working order. Early steam engines and flying machines
and bicycles; a printing shop, a tintype studio; a silk mill,
a gristmill and a windmill from Cape Cod; a smithy, a village firehouse, and an inn of the stagecoach days; the birth-
places of Henry Ford, William McGuffey, Luther Burbank,
and Orville Wright; the Illinois courthouse where Lincoln
practiced law; the house where Noah Webster wrote his
dictionary—all pass in review, to visitors' amazement and
delight: "All things are as they were then, except that you
are there."

The Singer Manufacturing Company, a staid and dignified enterprise for a hundred or so years, has taken up the
promotion trail with sewing-machine bees and fashion fes-
tivals to head off foreign competition. These sewing centers
are open to all comers throughout the United States and
Canada, with thousands of dollars in prizes going to those
who are most deft with the housewife's best friend. "The
Singer Sewing Machine Company," said John Morton, its
vice-president, "has survived so many international cata-
clysms that nothing short of a world-wide nudist movement
would frighten us."

The Fuller Brush Company, just turned fifty years, began business in a carriage shed in Hartford with a capital of
$375 and a first year's sales volume of $8,500; annual sales
now approach $100,000,000, achieved by door-to-door sales-
men recruited from the classified-advertising columns of the
daily newspapers. The Corning Museum of Glass at Corning, New York, has attracted some five million people from
every state in the Union and many foreign countries, providing in one place a complete picture of a single industry—

one of the earliest in America, founded at Jamestown, Virginia, in 1609. Other glass furnaces subsequently sprang up along the Atlantic seaboard. One of man's most versatile creations, glass articles were the first made-in-America commodities to be exported. The John W. Higgins Armory of the Worcester, Massachusetts, Pressed Steel Company, boasts a collection of ancient armor second only to that in the Tower of London. Business shrines have even invaded Disneyland, the Yale and Towne Company having set up on the main thoroughfare an old-time company lockshop, where Linus Yale, Jr., of Salisbury, Connecticut, devised the flat-key successor to the door latch and in which locks from ancient Egypt to our own day are on display. In the Library of Congress, 140,000 pages of Sears, Roebuck catalogues, from 1892, are recorded on microfilm—a sentimental journey through sixty-four years of fashions and foibles, comforts, and luxuries, household wares and whimsies. In the Museum of the Yonkers plant of the Otis Elevator Company, the first elevator built by the concern a century ago is demonstrated as a feature attraction.

The Home Insurance Company of New York maintains a popular collection of fire-fighting apparatus and equipment: an authentic replica of an 1800 firehouse, horse-drawn fire engines, hoses, axes, and trumpets. The Museum of Moneys of the World of the Chase-Manhattan Bank has an internationally famous collection of seventy-five thousand pieces on exhibit in New York. On the outskirts of Wilmington, Delaware, E. I. Du Pont de Nemours & Company is recreating in miniature the industries along Brandywine Creek which flourished a hundred and fifty years ago, by way of presenting a visual historical pageant of the country's industrial past through the medium of models, exhibits, and dioramas. Eleuthère Irénée Du Pont began making powder in the Brandywine area in 1802.

There are four infallible rules for a long and happy life for a business organization:

SHRINES OF FREE ENTERPRISE I

> To make products that are genuinely useful to people
> To make them better than others are making them
> To be the kind of company where good people like to
> work
> To have the good fortune to be a company doing business in a democracy.
> COLGATE-PALMOLIVE COMPANY, upon completion of
> its one-hundred-and-fiftieth year

> Nothing in *all history* has ever succeeded like America
> and every American knew it. Nowhere else on the globe
> had nature been at once so rich and so generous. The
> American was incurably optimistic . . . he believed that
> nothing was beyond his power, and was impatient with
> any success that was less than triumph. In every barefoot boy he saw a future president or a millionaire. Even
> his folk-lore—the Paul Bunyans and the Mike Finks—
> were of heroic mold.
> HENRY STEELE COMMAGER, *The American Mind;*
> Yale University Press, 1950.

SHRINES OF FREE ENTERPRISE—II

Research is an organized method for keeping you reasonably dissatisfied with what you have: intelligent ignorance is its first requirement. We should look back into the past and look forward and learn whatever we can because all the rest of our lives is going to be spent in the future. With willing hands and open minds, the future will be greater than the most fantastic story you can write. You will always underrate it.

CHARLES F. KETTERING, in *Collier's* (October, 1956)

The automobile is a fairly recent addition to American free enterprise. A person would have to be only fifty-nine years old to have ridden in the first American-made car when it was new. In that brief span, the motorcar has become the hallmark of necessity, convenience, and pleasure, fashioned for every man's purse and purpose. The industry has become a masterpiece of production, evolving from the tinkering in a woodshed half a century ago to the modern assembly line, with its undreamt of refinements and accessories. By way of recalling the days of the linen duster and retracing memory's macadam lane, the Horseless Carriage Club of Connecticut holds an annual rendezvous with an assemblage of a hundred ancient models, mechanically fit and shining bright, their names all but forgotten: Auburn, Ajax, Essex, Peerless, Lafayette, Pierce-Arrow, Saxon, Maxwell, Simplex, Rockne, Star; their places taken by sixty-two million modern counterparts of dazzling power and speed, all of them products of just five manufacturers. In 1900, there were only eight thousand vehicles registered.

Perhaps we should let the automobile tell its own story in its own words:

I am speed made subject to human will. I give mankind dominion over distance. I open the avenues of all the world to humanity. I enlarge the radius of human life. I expand the horizon of human opportunity. . . . I promote peace and good fellowship in the human race, for I have bridged the spaces that kept men isolated and ignorant of each other. . . . I snatch the dying from the scythe of death and outrun him a thousand times a day. . . . I save hours out of man's work-day and give them to him to play with. I make man free of all the far places of venture, recreation and delight. I am the most capable and constant servant in the homes of men. . . . I take men from their stifling cities of steel and stone out to the murmuring streams and windswept meadows. I cement the ties of home and kinship with the blessings of frequent reunion and concerted recreation. I give supremacy of locomotion to man whom nature made slower than the beasts. I am individual transportation free of all laborious limitations. . . . I am the Automobile.

JOHN O. MUNN (reprinted in *Gentry,* Fall, 1952)

At Saugus, Massachusetts, ten miles north of Boston on the Saugus River, the American Iron and Steel Institute has restored at a cost of more than a million dollars the iron works which flourished there three hundred years ago. Dating back to 1646, this birthplace of the industry, complete with blast furnace, forge, and a rolling mill, turned out hammers, saws, nails, axes, and sundry other articles and has become a place of public interest. Probably no other major industry has rediscovered and rebuilt its place of origin; the Saugus Works are considered the first successful producer of cast and wrought iron in the New World—an historic treasure and a shrine to private initiative and free enterprise. Some twenty thousand persons from every state visit the restoration annually.

It would be trifling with history, were we not to accord a conspicuous place in the making of modern America to the cotton gin—a device which exerted a profound influence upon the economic and social life of the nation, retrieving, as it did, the waning fortunes of the vast area in the Southland that we call "plantation America" and making possible the profitable culture and exploitation of an indispensable commodity. With Eli Whitney's device, one man could clean fifty pounds of cotton a day, as against a single pound by hand; in 1791, just before its adoption, the South was exporting 200,000 pounds of the staple a year; by 1807, this output had jumped to 63,000,000 pounds. Experimenting with revolutionary methods, machines, tools, and assemblies, Whitney also introduced the theory and practice of interchangeable parts, facilitating the manufacture of intricate mechanisms which do our work in countless different spheres—a principle that is recognized as a cornerstone of free enterprise.

When Phineas T. Barnum was not preoccupied by counting the clicks of his circus turnstiles, he was evidencing his faith in other business directions: in 1850 he founded the Pequonnock Bank in Bridgeport, Connecticut, which later merged with the Connecticut National. One of the oldest banking institutions in the United States, the latter began business in 1806 with a capital of $200,000; its assets today exceed $144,000,000. Barnum knew a thing or two about free enterprise!

Business executives are showing an ever-increasing interest in the corporate museum, evidencing pride in the development of their products over the years, promoting prestige and good will, and stimulating sales through the medium of attractive exhibits. In a recent survey of this relatively new field of business endeavor and imagination, the *Wall Street Journal* presented an extensive roster of firms engaging in this attention-getting sideline, among which are these:

The New York Trap Rock Corporation has converted a veteran scow into a floating museum on the Hudson, manned by company officials, which depicts the history of quarrying—

The Towle Manufacturing Company of Newburyport, Massachusetts, lends out its collection of fine old silverware to museums and jewelers—

Chicago's Felt and Tarrant Manufacturing Company devotes its array of calculating devices, some of them more than a hundred years old, to the training of its salesmen—

Baker Furniture, Inc., of Grand Rapids, Michigan, encourages visits to its display of museum pieces by students of decoration and design—

The Vermont Marble Company, at Proctor, maintains an exhibit of such company products as gravestones, bookends, bathrooms, doorsteps, rolling pins—

The International Business Machines Corporation has eighteen separate art collections on the road, including contemporary paintings from every country in which it does business—

The Waterbury Button Company of Waterbury, Connecticut, shows more than 100,000 different kinds of buttons—

General Motors has had as many as twenty-four trucks, convertible into outdoor exhibition stages, taking its collections on the road—

The Pennbrook Milk Company's museum in Philadelphia contains items relating to the dairy industry—

Museums with memorabilia of historic interest are maintained by a number of American railroads: the Farmer's Museum, across the road from Fenimore House, at Cooperstown, New York, contains a rare assortment of farm implements, wagons, looms, pottery, and dairy utensils used in New York State since colonial times. In operation as they were during frontier days are a smithy, a country store, a print shop, a one-room school, a law office, a pharmacy, and a farmhouse.

The world is only beginning to see that the wealth of a nation consists more than anything else in the number of superior men it harbors. In the practical realm it has always recognized this, and knows that no price is too high to pay for a great statesman or a great captain of industry. Today, America's great industries, under our system of free enterprise, are doing much to achieve this goal. Through grants to universities and colleges, private enterprise gives training to the nation's youth. Jobs requiring skill are open to young men and women as soon as they graduate, as are research facilities on a scale unknown in any previous age. In this way America is able to go forward in the highly competitive industrial and scientific world in which we live.

WILLIAM JAMES, *Memories and Studies;*
Longmans, Green and Co., 1917.

Science alone cannot guarantee security for civilization. Yet the problems facing man cannot be solved without science. Indeed, today man faces a thrilling opportunity as well as a great threat. The potentialities of science enable him to look bravely at the stars and to seek a finer destiny. He needs most the faith and the spiritual guidance that would lead him to apply his new knowledge to peaceful pursuits. For the hope of peace that is lasting and a world that is free lies within the soul, the heart, and the mind of man.

BRIG. GEN. DAVID SARNOFF in *Profile of America, An Autobiography of the U.S.A.*, edited by Emily Davie; Thomas Y. Crowell Co., 1954.

THE MIRACLE OF LIGHT

The history of the United States is fundamentally a history of invention. In itself, the United States was a new thing when it was devised. Consider for a moment what statesman, what soldier, what orator has changed the daily lives of men as much as the inventor of the electric light, the motion picture, the model T.

ROGER BURLINGAME, *Engines of Democracy;*
Scribner's, 1940.

Seventy years ago, the historian McMaster recounted the manifold improvements which had multiplied the conveniences of life and ministered to our happiness, and discussed the long series of mechanical inventions and discoveries which were the admiration of the world. Seventy years, as reckoned by history, is not very long; yet the mechanical marvels which Americans have contributed during the intervening years stagger the imagination, bringing with them a life of new horizons in leisure, recreation, and opportunity, all flourishing in the helpful climate of enlightened free enterprise—and with the promise of a still more wonderful era just ahead, as new wizards of the electronic age extend their reach and seek to grasp the undiscovered energies of the atom and the sun.

America having recently celebrated the diamond jubilee of light—the seventy-fifth anniversary of Thomas Alva Edison's invention, which ushered in civilization's indispensable servant—the Government has elected to include among its national shrines the laboratory and workshop at West Orange, New Jersey, where "the wizard of Menlo Park" conceived and perfected his many incredible inventions and devices. Charles Edison, son of the inventor, has deeded the land and buildings, and the contents will include a technical library of ten thousand volumes, and the original notebooks, blueprints, and working models of the phonograph, the incandescent lamp, motion-picture apparatus, the universal electric motor, the first electric railroad, a radically improved storage battery, various chemical applications, and many other artifices. Over a span of fifty years this self-tutored genius was to take out more than a thousand patents covering his varied conceptions, refinements, and improvements in a new and startling world of electricity, which, with his inquisitive and tireless mental and physical capacity, he was creating.

"What we are doing here," observed Edison's long-time friend and fellow scientist, Charles F. Kettering, "is dedicating the procedure by which ideas are pulled out of the wall of oblivion and made into things to serve humanity."

Born in 1847, this benefactor of civilization completed his "formal" education, of three month's duration, in the public school at Port Huron, Michigan. At the age of twelve he was a newsboy and "candy butcher" on the Grand Trunk Railway, studying and tinkering and experimenting in his spare time. As a reward for saving the life of the stationmaster's child, he was given lessons in telegraph operation at Mount Clemens and subsequently worked as an operator in various cities of the Middle West.

The phonograph, or, as it was first known, the "speaking machine," was among the earliest of Edison's triumphs destined to embellish our social and cultural environment. Observing that the surf, breaking on the beach, left undulations on the sand when the water receded, Edison concluded that with a suitable substance, sound waves could be made to trace their impressions with an embossing point. After a protracted trial and error, he wrapped tin foil tightly around a grooved cylinder that could be turned with a hand crank. Into this clumsy contraption he recited the familiar childhood jingle, "Mary Had a Little Lamb." When he proceeded with the playback, the diaphragm vibrated and repeated, faintly but distinctly, the words he had just spoken— to the utter amazement of his incredulous audience, who suspected a hidden ventriloquist. There followed a decade of unremitting research and constant improvement—the fabulous phonograph, the while, affording a major source of entertainment the world over.

But it was the incandescent lamp that was to establish beyond dispute Edison's place among the immortals. In 1879, after heartbreaking setbacks and costly failures, after a world-wide quest for an effective filament, the young "magician," groping with his fellow researchers in his home-made laboratory for this ultimate El Dorado, finally produced the bright, sustained glow of energy which ushered in civilization's most efficient handmaiden and transformed the ways of the world.

"To imprison the human spirit," writes W. MacNeile Dixon in *The Human Situation* (Longmans, Green & Co.), "is the unpardonable sin; to attempt to make men automatons, to force them into the same mold. No means will ever be found to induce human beings finally to surrender themselves, either body or soul, to a dictated felicity, to satisfactions chosen for them, whatever vulgar Caesars rule the world."

The annual production of electric lamps in the United States now exceeds two billion—enough to supply every person on earth with one bulb a year. Their efficiency is ten times as great and their cost of operation a fraction of that of the earlier, unrefined models.

In the novel field of talking motion pictures forty years ago, Edison, in association with Edwin S. Porter, made the first successful story film, *The Life of an American Fireman.* He capped his searching, restless career by serving as president of the Naval Consulting Board at the outbreak of the first World War, for which assignment he was awarded the Congressional Medal of Honor. He died at Glenmont, his home at West Orange, New Jersey, at the age of eighty-four, in 1931.

It is no exaggeration to talk about an American miracle. In a century and a half there has taken shape in North America a nation that is today one of the most powerful on earth. America has given its citizens more peace, stability and happiness than have any of the great nations of Europe. Tomorrow it will be, if it is well-informed, the world's greatest force in the service of justice.

ANDRE MAUROIS, *The Miracle of America;*
Harper's, 1944.

"EXCELSIOR"

One of the characteristics of American life is the extraordinary resilience and versatility with which the American people face new problems and adjust themselves to new situations. They don't like to accept things as they are, and to let people shift for themselves by dint of suffering and ingenuity. They prefer to change things and situations. They prefer to find a new arrangement, new equipment, a new gadget, a new line of social activity, for the sake of the human individuals involved.

JACQUES MARITAIN, *Reflections on America;*
Scribner's, 1958.

The George Eastman House of Photography at Rochester, New York, together with the one-story frame homestead moved from Waterville, which was his birthplace in 1854, stands as a memorial to the genius who heaped happiness on people everywhere by means of his Kodak, and later by his many benefactions—great and enduring contributions to the enrichment of community life. Here the visitor will find a rare collection of early motion pictures, bound sets of photographic magazines going back a hundred years, cameras, and technological material covering every aspect of the art of photography.

George Eastman's original experiments, conducted in his mother's kitchen sink, were to lead to the dry plate, the roll film, daylight loading, and finally the compact Kodak—"You Press the Button, We Do the Rest."

When asked the meaning of the word "Kodak," Eastman replied that "it doesn't mean a thing; but it's a good strong word, one that could not be misspelled or mispronounced, and could be registered as a trade-mark which would stand up against infringements."

Of the millions he amassed from his processes and inventions, Eastman dedicated much of his fortune to such worthy philanthropies as schools of medicine and of music at the University of Rochester, the Massachusetts Institute of Technology, the Hampton and Tuskegee Institutes for the advancement of colored people, and many other projects. Always living unostentatiously, George Eastman had little love for money except as an instrument for accomplishing worthy aims: "I have believed in trying to do some little things as I have gone along. I don't believe in men waiting until they are ready to die before using any of their money for helpful purposes."

That photography has become an important adjunct of everyday American life is attested by the fact that three out of every four American families each own one or more cameras, with which they snap over two billion pictures annually; an estimated five dollars of every one thousand dollars of "discretionary income" is spent on photographic products; and perhaps four million youngsters under eighteen years of age take up "shutter clicking" every year.

Constantly seeking refinements in the art, the Eastman Company lays great emphasis on research, toward which an annual budget of thirty-five million dollars is dedicated, some seventeen hundred scientists and technicians constantly working on new products and processes in the company's laboratories both in the United States and in a number of foreign countries.

Eastman's corporate history is one of America's most spectacular success stories. The inventor started business with six employees; the payroll now numbers some forty thousand, all of whom enjoy a comprehensive program of employee security. During the past ten years, sales have more than doubled, currently running around seven hundred million dollars, with earnings showing a similar impressive growth. The nine-hundred-acre Kodak Park in Rochester, with its more than one hundred major manufacturing buildings, is a living memorial to a self-made genius and generous benefactor as well as a shrine symbolic of free enterprise.

The priceless ingredient of the Eastman success story is its world-wide reputation for excellence. Every product must be *ne plus ultra* if it was expected to gain public acceptance. *Excelsior*—which is to say "of the highest order"—has long been the Eastman motto.

Seventy-five years ago, while working as a bank clerk in Rochester, Eastman devoted all of his spare time to photography and concluded that there must be room for improvement in the cumbersome equipment he encountered: the heavy nonportable camera, the darkroom, the wet plate, and the complicated developing routine. His commercial dry plate revolutionized the whole photographic process, reducing the early elaborate paraphernalia of photography to a minimum—to be followed by such other important innovations as the roll film and roll-holders to fit almost any style of camera, and these followed by the ever-popular Brownie.

Film still remains the company's chief product, of which there are some two hundred different kinds. A year's output of movie film alone would stretch to the moon and back, with enough left over to wrap several times around the equator of the earth! Other items in Eastman's amazing catalogue of "tricks" include movie cameras, projectors, color reproductions, synthetics and chemicals, and products in the fields of optics and electronics. And on the way is a new Minicard system, which combines the advantages of microfilm, punchcards, and digital computers.

In recognition of his commercial achievements, charitable contributions, and many boons to a more pleasureable existence, the United States Post Office in 1954 honored George Eastman by issuing a three-cent postage stamp with his likeness—one of the very few American businessmen thus recognized.

Nothing in the world can take the place of persistence. Talent will not; nothing is more common than unsuccessful men with talent. Genius will not; unrewarded genius is almost a proverb. Education will not; the world is full of educated derelicts. Persistence and determination alone are omnipotent. The slogan "Press on" has solved and always will solve the problem of the human race.

CALVIN COOLIDGE

THE EXEMPLAR

I love the man who can smile in trouble, who can gather strength from distress, and grow brave by reflection. 'Tis the business of little minds to shrink; but he whose heart is firm, and whose conscience approves his conduct, will pursue his principles unto death.

THOMAS PAINE (1737-1809)

It happens in every era that in our searchings for the truth, in our strivings for the high plateau, a leader we had so devoutly wished for had stood, too little recognized, always in our midst. The late Senator Robert A. Taft typified for millions the America we cherish, the embodiment of the faith of our fathers, the hope and aspirations of our sons: the unselfish servant, the respected opponent; the gracious winner, the gallant loser, accepting with equal grace the "slings and arrows of outrageous fortune" and a mortal affliction.

It is altogether fitting that on the Capitol grounds in Washington there will be reared a memorial to this public servant who, "born to integrity," never compromised his principles and whose character held the hallmark of courage. The Robert A. Taft Memorial Foundation has as its chairman Herbert Hoover and as its honorary chairman President Eisenhower.

"He had," as William S. White has written, "a luminous candor of purpose that was extraordinarily refreshing in a chamber not altogether devoted to candor."

Indicative of Taft's devotion to the common good was his deliberate choice, in 1947, of the chairmanship of the Labor Committee rather than that of the more prestige-laden Finance Committee—a choice he made because of his conviction that revisions of the Wagner Act were imperative. His deliberations in this direction led to his co-authorship in the Taft-Hartley Act, an espousal which incurred the enmity of labor and special-privilege groups. The legislation was passed over a presidential veto. In 1950 he was up for re-election to the Senate in his predominantly industrial state of Ohio, opposed by a heavily financed and well-trained organization capable of merciless attack upon him. Smaller men would have yielded to the apparently overwhelming odds. Taft eagerly accepted the challenge and won re-election.

"Liberalism," he had said, "implies particularly freedom of thought, freedom from orthodox dogma, the right of others to think differently from one's self. It implies a free mind, open to new ideas and a willingness to give attentive consideration. And liberty I take to mean liberty of the individual to think his own thoughts and live his own life as he desires to think and live."

Thrice thwarted—and grievously disappointed—in his ambitions for the Republican presidential nomination, he never allowed these frustrations to embitter him. Rather, he promptly closed ranks with his followers and threw all his influence behind Gen. Eisenhower's campaign and promptly pledged himself to the success of his administration.

Americans from far and near will be visiting the Taft Memorial to pay homage to this exemplar, a man of great distinction among the moderns, viewing the graceful shaft and hearing the carillon.

"At the turn of the century," wrote Senator John F. Kennedy in his admirable *Profiles in Courage* (Harper's), "the route to fame and power for men of ability and talent had been in industry, not in politics. And as a result, the attitude of the public toward the political profession had too often been characterized by apathy, indifference, disrespect and even amusement. The changing nature of the Senate, its work and its members, seems to have lessened the frequency with which the nation is given inspiration by a selfless stand for great but unpopular principles. Perhaps we are still too close in time to those in our own midst whose actions a more detached historical perspective may someday stamp as worthy of recording in the annals of political courage.

"Robert A. Taft stuck fast to the basic principles in which he believed. He was an able politician, but on more than one occasion he chose to speak out in defense of a position no politician with like ambitions would have endorsed. He was, moreover, a brilliant political analyst, yet he frequently flung to the winds the very restraints his own analysis advised, refusing to bow to any group, refusing to keep silent on any issue. He was known in the Senate as a man who never broke his agreement, who never compromised his deeply felt Republican principles, who never practiced political deception. It was these qualities, combined with an unflinching courage which he exhibited throughout his entire life, and most especially in his last days, that bound his adherents to him with unbreakable ties."

For this is the journey that men make; to find themselves. If they fail in this, it doesn't matter much what else they find. Money, position, fame, revenge, are all of little consequence, and when the tickets are collected at the end of the ride they are tossed into a bin marked Failure. But if a man knows what he can be depended upon to do, the limits of his courage, the position from which he will no longer retreat, the secret reservoirs of his determination, the extent of his dedication, his honest and unpostured goals—then he has found a mansion which he can inhabit with dignity all the days of his life.

JAMES MICHENER, *The Fires of Spring;*
Random House, 1949.

VALHALLAS OF THE IRON HORSE

All other scenes and sounds are pale and thin compared to the sight and the voice of the steam locomotive. As symbols of the United States, they are more accurate than the covered wagon or the echo of a homesteader's rifle. I think of them as unmistakenly American as the Flag and the Constitution.

STEWART H. HOLBROOK, *The Story of American Railroads;* Crown, 1947.

Many things that evoke glad associations have passed out of American life, giving place to modern invention: fire horses, street lamps, magic lanterns, ice wagons, wood-burning stoves, the family phaeton. Every man has his own particular nostalgia. And around the steam locomotive, now almost pushed into oblivion by the Diesel, has grown pride and affection, and romance, and tradition, to take rank among our most respected institutions—the spearhead of America's progress and expansion, the unifying bond of the nation.

In its heyday, the steam locomotive was the marvel of the age: nowhere else on earth were so many passengers and so much freight moving with such speed, regularity, and safety as in the United States—typifying America's giant strides toward economic usefulness and social development. "The rails running to the horizon," writes Lucius Beebe, "were indeed a royal road to romance, and a whole people rode them to far places and happy destinations both in fact and fancy. Manifest destiny lay around the curves and down the tangents." Its last "steamer"—Number 1977—has recently been scrapped by the New York Central, some two thousand Diesel units now taking care of the traffic rolling over the eleven thousand miles of track of the system. Indeed, hardly more than three thousand steam locomotives are currently operating in the entire United States.

Under the aegis of steam, every American had come to trust the familiar paraphrase from Herodotus: "Neither snow nor rain nor heat nor gloom of night stays these couriers from the swift completion of their appointed rounds." And a famed builder of railroad empires, James J. Hill, must have had these titans of locomotion in mind when he observed: "It is no exaggeration to say that in the history of this country, the railway—next after the Christian religion and the public schools—has been the greatest single contributing factor to the welfare and happiness of our people."

It is fitting that Baltimore was to become the first Valhalla of the Iron Horse, "the city of monuments" having established a permanent resting place for a well-preserved fleet of the forerunners of our modern motive power, an unequaled assembly dating back to 1829. These early "giants" of the rails are inscribed with their own distinctive names, missions, and capacities: *Tom Thumb, Atlantic, John Hancock, Lafayette* (the first locomotive with horizontal boiler), *Memon, William Mason, Thatcher Perkins,* the Davis *Camel, A. J. Cromwell,* the *Shay*—familiar nomenclature to everyone versed in American railway lore.

The graceful rotunda of the "round shop" of the Baltimore and Ohio Railroad at Mount Clare, with its twenty-
two tracks, houses this historic collection, which has become
a popular rendezvous for students, tourists, and historians.
The Mount Clare station is the oldest now standing anywhere; here the first tickets were sold for a regularly scheduled general-purpose train in 1830—the B and O's "flyer"
to Ellicott's Mills thirteen miles away; and from the ticket
agent's desk there was tapped out in 1844 and flashed to
Washington the first telegraph message—Samuel Morse's
prayerful phrase when he saw his dream of communication
by wire become a reality: "What hath God wrought!"

Also on display in the transportation museum is the
miniature "O"-gauge model railway. This is a spectacular
double-track mainline layout, complete and authentic in
every detail of equipment and operation. The diorama is
an actual reproduction of a scene along the Baltimore and
Ohio in the Potomac Valley.

Lesser shrines, too, keep us from forgetting these important facets of an early America on the march of progress.
Out in Ardmore, Oklahoma, Old 1108, with a million miles
on its driving rods, has been given to the city as a "conversa-
tion piece" for future generations. A city park at Tacoma,
Washington, has welcomed a proud old coal-burner with
all its vintage beauty, assuring it a more appropriate destiny
than the scrap heap. The Long Island Railroad's hundred-
ton Number 35, having earned a dignified retirement, will
pass its days on display at the Nassau Museum; to be followed, shortly, by the final trip of the last "steamer" of the
railroad to the Stony Brook Museum in Suffolk County. The
Southern Pacific Company has given an old steamer to the
city of Austin, Texas, where it will be on permanent display.
In some places the townsfolk have turned to and helped lay
the stretch of track for an old-timer to occupy. As nearly all
of America's sixty thousand steam locomotives are being
shunted off to sidings or are destined for destruction, civic

groups in many other cities are preparing retirement homes for the early trail-blazers.

Surviving also as a symbol of the age of steam will be a narrow-gauger brought down from the Yukon, after forty-eight years of service, to take its place in history in the Black Hills of South Dakota. It will supplement the rolling stock of the Black Hills Central, which will cover the run from Hill City to a mountaintop clearing called Oblivion, where the "history train" makes a turn-around. Gov. Foss has hailed the venture as a "sincere effort on the part of a group of dedicated railroad men to preserve a working steam railroad for persons of all ages who share America's fondness for the rapidly vanishing steam locomotive." To show their affection for the frontier train, visitors from all over the country flock to Durango, Colorado, to ride the last regularly scheduled narrow-gauge passenger train in America—a rugged run of forty-five miles on the Silverton Branch of the Denver and Rio Grande.

A Valhalla where two famous warriors of the rails came together in triumphant union—Promontory, Utah, 1,086 miles west of the Missouri River and 690 east of Sacramento —is being set aside by the Department of the Interior as the Golden Spike National Historical Site, to be restored, with appropriate mementos and administered by the National Park Service. Here, on May 10, 1869, the wood-burning *Jupiter* of the Central Pacific Railroad and the coal-burning engine Number 119 of the Union Pacific made gentle contact, effecting a clasp of steel between East and West. The Spike, inscribed in 1863, when the great link was first begun, was driven home by Gov. Leland Stanford and, now reposing in a San Francisco bank vault, bears the legend: "May God continue the unity of our country as this railroad unites the two great oceans of the world."

A Glencoe, Illinois, sales executive Earl J. Witt, haunted by the recent demise of the Hooppole, Yorktown, and Tampico line which used to ramble along a 120-mile stretch of Illinois countryside, has formed a committee "for the Preservation of the Steam Locomotive for Posterity," so that the people of Chicago may know what a "steamer" looked like, even if they never hear its lonesome wail, which is fast giving way to the throaty grunt of the Diesel. To assuage the loneliness of nostalgic airmen stationed in the Iceland outposts, the Canadian National Railways is dispatching a king-sized locomotive whistle, which it is hoped will dispel, as nothing else would, the prevailing melancholia.

A new railroad museum known as Rail City has been opened at Sandy Creek, New York, with steam trains in actual operation, where the visitor can "get the feel" of what railroading was like in the good old days.

It appears that the steam locomotive is on the way out, and so into limbo with the Concord Coach and the Erie Canal. There is no use protesting against its going. The Diesel is nothing to offer a man in place of the classic Iron Horse that spanned the continent in less than a man's lifetime, bound it with arteries that carried the blood of life into its most remote and inaccessible parts—that tamed its wildness, softened its savagery, and civilized its places and peoples as nothing else could have done. All this was done so quickly that the world of reflective men has not yet ceased to marvel.

> STEWART H. HOLBROOK, *The Story of American Railroads;* Crown, 1947.

In the century and a quarter lifespan of steam power, no artifact was more characteristic of the American way of life than the steam railroad engine. No American lived who was not affected by it; none saw or experienced it without being moved by its implications of combined beauty and usefulness.

> LUCIUS BEEBE & CHARLES CLEGG, *The Age of Steam;*
> Rinehart, 1958.

SHRINES OF SPORT

It is more and more widely recognized that what a nation does with its *leisure* is oftentimes just as significant as how it either maintains itself economically or governs itself. The traditional patterns of every-day living have been completely altered with an ever growing need for play that can effectively compensate for the intensity under which we work. If many of the forms of recreation which have evolved under these circumstances appear far from ideal, one wonders what the urban masses would be doing if they did not have their commercial amusements and spectator sports.

FOSTER RHEA DULLES, *America Learns to Play;*
Appleton, 1940.

Every spring, Americans come out of hibernation for six months and contract a raging baseball fever, plunge into hysterics and prostration, urging on their favorites to surpassing feats, comparing notes as to how the winter trades are turning out, and following the fortunes of that "bonus" boy from the bushes. Close upon the thrilling strains of the national anthem ranks the annual clarion call "Play ball!"

This sporting enthusiasm has been going on in varying degrees of frenzy ever since organized baseball began in 1845 under the auspices of the Knickerbocker Club of New York, soon to be joined by teams representing Brooklyn, Philadelphia, and other cities. These informal intercity contests took on an amateur flavor at the start and were played on the Elysian fields in Hoboken, then a fashionable resort, drawing their patronage largely from the upper echelons of society. Baseball became a national sport during the Civil War, when it was introduced by northern soldiers to men from other sections of the country. Indeed, a forerunner of baseball is said to have been played by men of Gen. Washington's army during the Revolutionary War. During both World Wars, the game was taken up by a number of other nations, achieving its greatest popularity in Japan.

Having won recognition by the public as America's national game, baseball has a commemorative Hall of Fame all its own—the first of many shrines of sport which were to follow: racing's Hall of Fame and National Museum at Saratoga honors twelve leading jockeys, six trainers, and ten of the most outstanding thoroughbreds, all of whom raced prior to 1900; the Jockeys' Hall of Fame at Pimlico, Maryland, whose first choices for the distinction were Eddie Arcaro, Earl Sande, and George Woolf, recently followed by Johnny Longden, Tod Sloan, and Isaac Murphy, with others to be added each year as a result of popular polling; at the Tennis Hall of Fame at the Newport Casino, the late Dwight Davis and seven other "immortals" of the courts were lately enshrined; the Golf House and Museum on 38th Street in Manhattan has been established as headquarters for anything anybody wants to know about "the royal and ancient game" and the modern and very popular game. Starting in this country with the nine-hole course of the Oakhurst Club in West Virginia in 1884, the game now embraces five thousand layouts covering about a thousand square miles of land, with six hundred thousand members who spend some $150,000,000 on the sport every year. And down in Texas, Dallas has a Sports Hall of Fame all its own, having recently inducted Cecil Smith—Mr. Polo—who has been a ten-goal player for twenty years. At the age of fifty-two, Smith's is still the greatest name in polo—a legend along with that of the late Tommy Hitchcock.

Located at Cooperstown, New York, a small rural community on the tip of Lake Otsego, a site in keeping with the origin of the sport which first saw action on sandlots and pastures and village greens, baseball's Hall of Fame was dedicated as the birthplace of the game when its doors were thrown open to the public June 12, 1939, when the original thirteen "selectmen" were inducted: Hans Wagner, Napoleon Lajoie, Cy Young, Ty Cobb, Grover Alexander, Tris Speaker, Christy Mathewson, Willie Keeler, Walter Johnson, Connie Mack, George Sisler, Babe Ruth, Eddie Collins. The present roster, chosen by a poll of baseball writers, honors with bronze plaques an enrollment of eighty-three acclaimed as the game's immortals. Included also are deans and dignitaries and umpires chosen for their meritorious service: Morgan G. Bulkley, first National League president; Ban Johnson, first American League president; Henry Chadwick, pioneer, chronicler, and statistician; A. G. Spalding, veteran player and founder of the sporting-goods firm; Judge Kenesaw M. Landis, baseball's first commissioner; William Klem, with the National League umpiring staff for forty-six years; Thomas Connally, of the American League staff for fifty-two years.

President William Howard Taft was the first President to throw out the first ball, opening the 1909 season. Every President since then has carried on the custom, giving baseball the official sanction as the national pastime, a status further attested by the thousands of fans who are lured each year to the museum at Cooperstown, where there is assembled the most complete collection of baseball memorabilia, records, relics, books, pictures, equipment, uniforms, covering the history and development of the game from its early days to modern times.

While the first scheme for playing baseball is reckoned to have been devised by Abner Doubleday at Cooperstown in 1839, history is a little hesitant about bestowing the accolade of "Father of Modern Baseball" between him and Alexander Joy Cartwright, Sr. The latter gentleman—a surveyor—worked out the ninety-foot spacings between bases on the theory that a grounder handled cleanly by an infielder and thrown to first should beat the runner by a fraction of a second. After a hundred years of play, this is still the accepted measurement. Cartwright is also said to have established nine innings as a regular game and nine players as a team.

Who ever wants to know the heart and mind of America had better learn baseball, the rules and realities of the game. Baseball fitly expresses the powers of the nation's mind and body; it is the most active, agile, varied, articulate, and brainy of all group games; it is of and for our century. Accuracy and speed, the practiced eye and hefty arm, the mind to take in and readjust to the unexpected, the possession of more than one talent and the willingness to work in harness without special order— these are the American virtues that shine in baseball. The rules keep pace with this imaginative creation so rich in allusions to real life: a victory has to be won, not snatched; just as near the end of any struggle, life asks for more than is needful in order to clinch success. Even the man in the bleachers is enjoying a spectacle that the gods on Olympus contrived only with difficulty when they sent Helen to Troy and picked their teams. And for those whom civilized play doesn't fully satisfy, there has been provided a scapegoat in a blue suit—the umpire—yellproof and as even-handed as justice.

JACQUES BARZUN, *God's Country and Mine;*
Little, Brown & Co., 1954.

"THE CITADEL OF PROMISE"

New York is notoriously the largest and least loved of
any of our great cities. Why should it be loved as a city?
It is never the same city for a dozen years together. A
man born forty years ago finds nothing of the New York
he knew. The landmarks, the objects which marked the
city to him, as a city, are gone. We are not yet eighty
years old as a nation, and there is scarcely one historic
house left standing in our greatest city. New York might
rattle about our ears tomorrow; but who, if he had his
family safe and were well insured, would care? (quoted
in the *New York Times Book Review*) —*Harper's New
Monthly Magazine,* July, 1856

If *Harper's* roving reporter of a hundred years ago were
covering Manhattan today, he might tell a different story.
By present-day comparisons there are lots of antiquities
in and around New York, but they take a little looking for,
what with all the hustle and bustle and Babel, and one's

amazement at modern marvels. The first capital of the United States, until 1790, and capital of the state until 1797, New York boasts of a variety of "firsts": Fulton's first practical steamboat, the *Clermont,* went up the Hudson from New York to Albany in 1807 in thirty-two hours; the first horse railroad in the world started its run along Fourth Avenue in 1832. Apart from its wealth of historic sites and associations, the city is replete with galleries and museums, libraries, and churches, parks and zoos and botanical gardens, philanthropies and ferryboats and memorials.

A metropolis of more than eight million people, it is the most populous Italian city outside of Italy; it is the world's third-largest Irish city, the world's greatest Negro center, and the foremost city of Jews. It is the home of thousands of people of French origin and of German extraction, and of thousands of others who preserve in some degree the customs of China, Syria, of Greece and Russia, and of many other Old World peoples.

"There has never been any clear-cut claimant to the land making up the United States of America. Columbus was an Italian sailing for Spain; Cabot was an Italian in the service of England; Hudson was an Englishman employed by the Dutch; Cabrillo was a Portuguese working for Spain; Amerigo Vespucci was an Italian commissioned by Portugal. This country has become in actual fact a land of freedom for all races, colors and creeds." (Emerson M. Brooks, *The Growth of a Nation;* Dutton)

New Yorkers flock in the summertime to their first love, Battery Park, to rest by the sea, and to recall the memories of Castle Garden, where Lafayette and Albert Edward, Prince of Wales, received their first welcomes to our shores, and where Jenny Lind, the Swedish nightingale, came to captivate her listeners under the auspices of Phineas Barnum, and where the deal was closed with the Indians for the Purchase of Manhattan for twenty-four dollars. It was first converted to an immigrant station which received millions of new arrivals, and then to a mammoth aquarium; plans are now afoot to rebuild what remains of the original Castle Clinton.

Unique in its purpose and design, the Cooper Union for the Advancement of Science and Art, completed in 1858 at Seventh Street and Fourth Avenue, was the forerunner both of skyscraper construction and of democratic education. Manufacturer, ironmaster, and philanthropist, its founder Peter Cooper provided free forum lectures, classes, and concerts with a view "to aiding the efforts of youth in acquiring that kind of useful knowledge which will enable them to find and fill valuable places to the greatest possible advantage to themselves and the community." Lincoln made his memorable Cooper Union address here in 1860, and twelve other Presidents have spoken in the great hall.

New York's City Hotel, opened in 1794, was the first building erected in America for the purpose of offering accommodations after the manner of our present-day establishments. It stood, with its seventy-three rooms, below Trinity Church in Broadway and promptly catered to distinguished visitors and became the center of the city's social life. Another housing relic is the old five-story brick building in 18th Street between Third Avenue and Irving Place—the first modern apartment building in the United States. Dating from 1869, it is still doing business. Immediately after his inauguration as first President, George Washington attended services at St. Paul's Chapel, the oldest church structure in New York, in Church Street. Still holding out against a forest of sky-piercing towers is Cleopatra's Needle, the Egyptian obelisk in back of the Metropolitan Museum in Central Park, said to date from 1500 B.C. One of the largest and most important private collections of early-American sheet music in existence is to be found in the New York Public Library: a first American printing of "Yankee Doodle," the marching song of the Revolutionary War printed in 1795; two title pages illustrated by James McNeill Whistler for "The Song of the Graduates," dated 1582 and executed by the artist while he was a cadet at West Point; a cover by Winslow Homer; a first edition of "Hail, Columbia," our first national anthem; and a number of early printings of "The Star-spangled Banner." Among the rarities to be found in the New York Historical Society, at Central Park West, are the city's first newspaper, the *Gazette*, beginning in 1730, copies of every New York City directory from 1786, the original articles of Burgoyne's surrender, an orderly-book record of the execution of Nathan Hale, and some two hundred letters of George Washington.

The New York Stock Exchange has recently completed, at a cost of a million dollars, an exhibition hall and visitor's gallery at 20 Broad Street—an animated replica of the exchange and its operation. Seventeen major exhibits are presented, most of them operated by prominent corporations whose securities are listed on the big board.

Out near the tip of Long Island, at Easthampton, the Old Mulford Farmhouse, nearly three hundred years old, has been restored by the local citizenry. Best known of the prolific clan was Samuel Mulford—"Old Fishhooks"—a sobriquet he earned when, upon being despatched by the colonists to England to plead with the King for a reduction in the tax on whale oil, stuffed his pockets with fishhooks against London night prowlers.

If the efforts of certain foundations and a group of public-spirited citizens are successful, Hamilton Grange, the New York City home of Alexander Hamilton which has been officially designated as an historic site especially worthy of preservation, will be restored, refurnished, and moved from its present blighted location to a rural setting on the wooded campus of Manhattanville College. Born in the British West Indies two hundred years ago, Hamilton served as first Secretary of the Treasury, 1789-95, and was the founder of the United States Coast Guard, formerly known as the Revenue Cutter Service. Thus will be appropriately honored the memory of one of America's most useful and devoted sons.

The American, whether he chooses to work on his farm or behind a bench in town or behind a desk in the city, represents the dignity of the individual that is reflected in all of our basic American documents. When free men give up their individual dignity in favor of state-given security, when the incentives this freedom provides are in any way tampered with, then man becomes totalitarian, production declines, the consumer gets less and the commissars send delegates to the free countries to learn their secret.

HENRY T. McKNIGHT, former President of The Council for Agricultural and Chemergic Research

The cynic may say that the American city has no heart, the country no head, and the suburb no soul. But such a picture will not stand analysis. When the breakfast-table radio announces that a freckled-faced kid has lost a mongrel dog, a hundred thousand heartless city dwellers set out to find the pooch; readers of *Walden* will discover how much food for thought a city man can find sitting by a rural pond; and anyone who has attended an evening meeting of a suburban village board will have to admit that the tired commuter has something on his mind more compelling than escape from the city.

ROBERT MOSES; New York City Park Commissioner.

THE END OF THE SAWDUST TRAIL

We cannot believe that this is the end of the circus. We would as readily give up our faith in Santa Claus, or doubt the existence of good fairies. The circus was the one dependable harbinger of spring. In an ever-changing world it was the abiding certainty. If this, too, passes, what else in our world can be considered safe from extinction? Are we to have an age ahead when small boys have never carried water to elephants, or sneaked under a tent, or smelled the glorious—and some not so glorious —smells of the circus? Is there no way to halt the march of mechanization, of air-conditioning? What is progress, the world of tomorrow, without a circus?

New York *Times*

Sadness came to young America—and to old America, too, for that matter—with the announcement from John Ringling North that for a variety of economic reasons he had been obliged to fold the biggest of the big tops. "The tented circus as it has existed," he said, "has become a thing of the past." Its visits will be limited to the big-city sports arenas.

No more will youngsters bask in the fine, free world of fantasy and oldsters experience their annual rejuvenation and escape from global hurly-burly when the circus brought its wondrous panoply to town—with its new acts, new animals, new accessories, and, of course, new adjectives. In the words of Ernest Hemingway, the circus is "the only ageless delight that you can buy for money—the only spectacle I know that while you watch it, gives the quality of a truly happy dream."

It is a little saddening, too, to realize that a full generation of Americans has reached maturity without ever having thrilled to that gay and gaudy spectacle, the circus parade, which did so much to enliven the American scene for the fifty years between 1880 and 1930; to think that so many present-day folk were missing from those happy throngs which stood for hours along the curb on Main Street waiting in hushed, starry-eyed anticipation for the dazzling splendor of the pageant.

Then, of a sudden, the word would spread: "Here it comes! The parade is coming! Hold your horses, the elephants are coming"; and presently there was to pass in review a mile of "gleam, gold and glamour": the leading band carriage with its forty-horse hitch, prancing four abreast; the colorful circus wagons, with their frightening freight of beasts of prey; acrobats and bareback riders and funnymen; floats and tableaux drawn by caparisoned percherons, depicting the storied kingdom of make-believe; the steam calliope, with its thirty shrieking whistles, bringing up the rear.

But if the press of circumstance has forced the abandonment of the pomp and thrill of the circus parade from its accustomed lines of march, the spirit of the big top has been faithfully preserved in authentic memorials. There is the Museum of the American Circus, set up in the former Ringling residence at Sarasota, Florida, where the big show has its winter quarters. Here are on view the old parade wagons, lithographs, bill posters, and historical material, the spangles and trappings and paraphernalia of the canvas caravan. At Somers, New York, considered the birthplace of the American circus, another shrine has taken shape, featuring TIP— one of the largest and most ferocious Indian elephants ever taken into captivity—now stuffed and quite harmless but the recipient of a rousing reception by the townsfolk. It was here, also, that Hackaliah Bailey exhibited Old Bet, known as the first elephant to arrive in this country. He built the Elephant Hotel, now the Somers Town Hall, with Old Bet's earnings. And at the New York Historical Society there was lately held an exhibit of "Thumbiana"—a one-man show concerning itself with Mr. Charles Sherwood Stratton, of Bridgeport, Connecticut, affectionately known in his day from one end of the land to the other as Tom Thumb, the mightiest midget. Under P. T. Barnum's auspices, he was the smash hit of the show, the darling of the sawdust world at home and abroad, cavorting with a martial air and in Union Army regalia. He departed the world of the giants, of apoplexy, at the age of forty-five.

And surely there should be a shrine to the clown, for he is the heart of the circus, drawing the "cleansing lash of laughter" upon all his works and wiles. The Irish essayist John Sheridan has fixed the place of the clown high in the circus firmament: "The clown gives us back a sense of perspective that children have as a birthright and grow out of as they grow up; for it blurs quickly under the necessity of that tiresome discipline known as law and order. In the circus, as in the world, there is always someone to crack the whip, and he is the clown's natural enemy. The ringmaster may shine with oil and white linen but he is as unpopular as a regimental sergeant-major: he stands for the police, and income tax notices, and pomposity, and human respect. So our hearts go out to the clown when he thumbs his nose at authority, and we revel by proxy for an hour or two at his antics."

The circus is a creature of fact and fantasy—of imperishable fantasy—of experience, age and perpetual youth. Its father was a charioteer; its mother, a juggler. It took its first steps in an open ring, spent its youth on a galloping horse, and grew to maturity in a tent. The swift and dramatic spectacle we call circus is so suited to the American temperament that it seems to us typically our own. Nevertheless, it is ours only by adoption, for it first acquired form and vitality in London. Philip Astley, an eighteenth-century British trick rider, is called Father of the Circus. In its essence the circus is the most ancient and persistently popular form of entertainment devised by man. When primitive man, first controlling his lust to kill, took home a wild animal and made a pet of it, the menagerie began. The person who first exploited the abnormality of some other human being anticipated the side show. The first pagan priest who arranged a procession in honor of his god was the true originator of the circus parade.

MARIAN MURRAY, *Circus! From Rome to Ringling;*
Appleton, 1956.

THE UNDERWORLD

Though caves existed long before man, and have been used by man since he appeared on this planet, they are still a frontier—in a sense, the last frontier. The adventure into darkness is on—into darkness that is total, but hides some of the rarest beauties that ever dazzled disbelieving eyes. Many more than a million Americans each year experience the awe and delight of the eerie underworld, visiting the comparatively small number of caves that have been prepared for public view. And a growing band of hardy souls is constantly pushing back the subterranean horizon. They are the spelunkers—the cave crawlers—who go on and on where no human being has ever been before, or perhaps where men have forgotten to go for millennia, and where priceless relics of the human past lie waiting to be discovered.

FRANKLIN FOLSOM, *Exploring American Caves;*

Crown, 1956.

Authorities estimate that there are more than five thousand known caves in the United States, but seasoned spelunkers believe there must be fifty thousand other caves and caverns and grottoes scattered through practically every state in the Union awaiting the explorer's invasion of the closely guarded mysteries of the underground labyrinths: the fantastic formations of rocks and fissures, stalagmites and stalactites, forbidding gullies and spectacular waterfalls, lakes, and rivers that Charon might have crossed in his "crazy Stygian wherry." Holes in the ground have always had a fascination for the inquisitive, both young and old. A few miles down the Mississippi from Hannibal, Missouri, Tom Sawyer's intrepid adventures invariably brought him to the Mark Twain Cave—the most exciting rendezvous of all. In the town's Riverside Park, incidentally, the great humorists's statue bears the fitting inscription: "His religion was humanity, and a whole world mourned for him when he died." And maybe around the river bend one could have heard the steamboat's leadsman calling off the water's depth: M-A-R-K Twain! Indeed, "the American nation came to birth upon the rivers. Are we a restless people because motion flowed by us continuously in our youth? Are we optimistic, eager, imaginative, daring, and even recklessly experimental because of the beckoning of the tides which ran swiftly past our known shores into domains beyond our vision?"

Mammoth Cave, in southwestern Kentucky, discovered about a hundred and fifty years ago by a hunter who stalked a wounded bear into what proved to be its entrance, is still the patriarch of the cave world, the first commercial cave in America and a tourist attraction second only to Niagara Falls. Now a National Park embracing some fifty thousand acres, it is ten miles in circumference, and its Echo River is 360 feet below the surface. In the War of 1812, it was a source of saltpeter, used in the manufacture of munitions; a hundred years ago it was set up as a tuberculosis sanitorium but the experiment was quickly abandoned when the patients did not prosper. Near by is the Sand or Crystal Cave which Floyd Collins encountered on one of his many expeditions of discovery, only to be pinioned in one of its treacherous recesses. Gallant rescue efforts were unavailing and he died a martyr to his mission into the unknown after what must have seemed an eternity of agony.

Carlsbad Caverns, hidden under the desert in southeastern New Mexico, off the beaten path of population, was discovered in 1911 by a cowboy, Jim White, and was later named a National Park by President Coolidge. Half a million persons make the trek every year to marvel at the majesty and immensity of these awesome natural wonders. An elevator takes the visitors to the huge underground dining room 750 feet below the surface. Nor have the caverns given up all their secrets: their vastness will yield only to time and travail and patient exploration. Meanwhile, millions of people are learning something about the "grandeur and complexity of the world's evolution" through the persistence and curiosity of a young range-rider who could neither read nor write.

"Legend has it," writes Mr. Folsom, "that sometime late in the eighteenth century, as the frontier began to reach the boundaries of Indiana, a nameless pioneer nursed a nameless wounded Indian back to health. To show his gratitude, the patient led the pioneer to Wyandotte Cave, not far from the spot where the Blue River enters the Ohio." Thus began the white man's acquaintanceship with this great cave which Indians had known and used for many centuries: Wyandotte Cave, near the town of Leavenworth, is the third-largest in the United States. Meanwhile, folks in the Shenandoah Valley of Virginia had become cave-conscious, lured chiefly by an underground boat ride in the Howe Caverns. Then came the discovery of Luray Caverns near New Market—probably the most beautiful of the American underground systems, with evidences of the antiquity of man on this continent in the form of human bones embedded in the flowstone.

A ten-week excavation jointly sponsored by the National Geographic Society and the Smithsonian Institution recently uncovered in Russell Cave in Alabama "a consecutive record of human occupancy from about 6,000 B.C. until approximately 1650 A.D." No other site in North America has yielded a detailed record covering so long a time. It is located close to Bridgeport, near the Tennessee border. Stone points, bone tools, potsherds, shell ornaments, and telltale charcoal from man-made fires are said to carry the human story in early America forward from the Stone Age until thirty years after the Pilgrims landed.

The cave was man's first natural home; some atomic-age pundits fear that it may also be his last. Oddly, however, though man has probed earth's atmosphere, mapped its surface, scaled its highest peaks and scraped its ocean bottoms, he has largely neglected the myriad subterranean realms. Mountaineering has its classic literature, but caves—mysterious, magnificent and challenging as mountains—still await their authors. Poet-novelist Folsom in his *Exploring American Caves* with its bold plunge into virtually virgin writing territory may prove to be classic cave literature.

Time magazine, July 9, 1956

THE GREATEST LOVE

Magnanimity includes all that belongs to a great soul; a high and mighty courage, an invincible patience, and immovable grandeur which is above the reach of injuries, a certain kind of majesty that is conversant with great things; a high and lofty frame of spirit, an infinite hope and a vast desire; a generous confidence and a great inclination to heroic deeds.

THOMAS TRAHERNE (1636-74)

At National Memorial Park in Falls Church, Virginia, not far from the national capital, a graceful commemorative fountain honors the four American chaplains who in World War II went down with the torpedoed troopship *Dorchester* off the Greenland coast, after having given up their life jackets, that four soldiers might survive:

GEORGE LANSING FOX, Methodist minister, called to duty from a snowbound parish in Vermont

234

ALEXANDER DAVID GOODE, the able and popular young
rabbi from a synagogue in rural Pennsylvania
CLARK V. POLING, the well-loved Dutch Reformed pastor,
quitting a comfortable assignment in upstate New York
JOHN PATRICK WASHINGTON, the greatly respected Catholic priest, born and bred in industrial New Jersey

It is a shrine dedicated to courage and selflessness and honor,
recalling for our edification one of the unforgettable sagas
of the sea.

Constantly ministering to the lonely, homesick lads below decks, where time tormented the soul and preyed upon
the nerves, these four servants of the Lord gave some the
strength to live, others the courage to die; and they gave to
all of them the noble example of self-effacement, Christian
resignation, the fatherhood of God, the brotherhood of man.

The unselfish epic has been recounted with great poig-
nancy and deep understanding by Francis B. Thornton,
himself a chaplain in the first World War, in his admirable
narrative, *Sea of Glory* (Prentice-Hall) , a heartening odyssey
dedicated to all men who have died for their country:

"The transport rose and fell sluggishly at her pier, her
lines alternately slack and tight. In the darkness beneath
the flooring, down at the water-line of the rusty ship, there
was the slap of the waves against her sides and against the
pilings—one of the loneliest sounds that can haunt man's
ears. Soldiers climbing the gangplank looked at the *Dorchester* as though they had been cheated in a poker game
even before the cards were dealt: she was an old work-horse
of the sea, intended to carry slow cargo in her crowded holds,
given to pitching and rolling even in good weather, and to
yawing crazily in heavy seas. Whatever dignity she was to
possess would have to go aboard her in the hearts and breasts
of the soldiers using her as a ferry to the bloody fields of
war; she had none of her own.

"Historians could speak of her gangplank in later years
as a bridge to man's victory against the forces of totalitarian

evil. It was a narrow, unstable link between the known
and the unknown, between the safety of the shore and home
and the awful dangers of the sea. Each man, tired and cold
as he was that January night, must have thought about it as
he plodded up the incline and stepped upon the steel plates
of the freighter's deck. The men's faces were bleak, as only
fighting men's faces can be, shoving off for overseas or moving out on a patrol. It's the eyes that tell the story. The
healthy glint that is any man's birthright grows lacklustre
on the eve of battle or danger; the sockets become a little
deeper, stretching the skin into shadowed crowsfeet. So it
was with these men coming aboard the *Dorchester*. They
could only guess at the future.

"The days were bad enough, but the nights were empty
voids of terror for many of the soldiers. Small lights in the
holds, casting their eerie blue brightness, were no compensa-
tion for the blackness that enshrouded the whole convoy.
Dangers that could be seen were bad enough—those that
couldn't be were like icy fingers on a man's lungs. And
always there was the lurching and the endless creaking of
the deck girders and the bulkheads. The North Atlantic
was then perhaps the bitterest battleground of all the fronts."

Somewhere up ahead, well north of the great circle route,
in the "impatient wilderness of the ocean," destiny was
altering the *Dorchester*'s course to a rendezvous with history,
when out of the night's brittle silence a torpedo dealt the
helpless hulk a mortal blow. The ship's bells struck twice;
it was one o'clock in the morning. They never sounded again;
the siren shrieked its last alarm.

The four men of God stood solemnly at the rail of the
lunging deck, arms linked, eyes upraised, each with the
prayer of his faith on his lips:

"Our Father, which art in heaven . . ."

"In nomine Patris, et filii, et Spiritus Sancti . . ."

"Hear, O Israel, the Lord our God, the Lord is one . . ."

"Forgive us our trespasses as we forgive those . . ."

In the terror and confusion, a lad sent up an agonizing appeal to one of the four; which one, it doesn't matter—each one gave his life belt to a soldier.

"Padre, padre, I've lost my life jacket and I can't swim. I'll . . ."

"Take mine," the reassuring answer came back; "I'm staying. I won't need it."

"God bless you," the lad whispered as he crawled into the sea.

It was Emerson who admonished us "never to lose an opportunity of recognizing anything that is beautiful; for Beauty is God's handwriting—a wayside sacrament. Welcome it in every fair face, in every fair sky, in every fair flower."

Here, indeed, stood beauty—beauty of the spirit, beauty of the soul, beauty of the Psalm: "Greater love hath no man than this that he lay down his life for a friend." Heroism? Duty? Consecration? We might grope till doomsday to find the word that best befits those four patriot-priests— Protestant, Catholic, and Jew—who gave the last full measure of devotion on a voyage of destiny and martyrdom. And the last words of the dying Stonewall Jackson might well become every hero: "Let us cross over the river, and rest under the shade of the trees."

How simple then is our duty; loyalty to life, to the ship's company, and to ourselves. I like to think that men are machines of a celestial pattern, which can rise above themselves, and to the amazement of the watching gods acquit themselves as men.

W. MacNeile Dixon, *The Human Situation;*
Longmans, 1937.

"Successive generations of young men know that theirs is truly a breathtaking heritage, and that were their entire lives required to preserve it, whether by dying for it as some young men tragically have, the span would be all too short and the sacrifice none too great. From all of our faiths blended together there is distilled a universal quality, an America that is like no other country in history, an America that can become both great and eternal."

CLARENCE B. RANDALL

Freedom's Faith; Little, Brown and Company, 1953.

Bless us, O Almighty God, Creator of heaven and earth, and grant us to be humble under Thy generous hand. Without Thee we can do nothing, but can do all things in Thee who strengthenest us. Thou hast made man a little less than the angels, hast crowned him with glory and honor, and hast placed him over all the works of Thy Hands. Give us wisdom ever to be conscious of our stewardship, to live and labor for the betterment of man to the glory of Thy name.

REV. T. M. HESBURG, C.S.C.;

President, University of Notre Dame

INDEX

A

Adams, Henry, 165
Alamo, The, 92
Allen, Durwood, L., 125
American Circus Museum, 227
American Legion Resolution, 150
American Museum of Immigration, 42
Anderson, Robert B., 135
Andrews, Dr. Charles M., 35
Arizona National Monuments and Museums, 93-94
Arlington House, Va., 28
Audubon, John James, 80

B

Bailey, Thomas A., 162
Bakeless, John, 87
Baldwin, Leland DeWitt, 108-109
Barton, William, 127
Barzun, Jacques, 220
Baseball Hall of Fame, Cooperstown, N. Y., 219
Beard, Daniel Carter, 123
Berger, Josef and Dorothy, 109
Billington, Ray Allen, 105
Biloxi, Miss., 74
Botkin, B. A., 73
Bowles, Samuel, 139
Bradford, William, 32
Brooks, Emerson M., 221
Brown, Henry Armitt, 9
Brown, John, 30

Bruckberger, Rev. R. L., 50
Buffalo Bill's Wild West Show, 168
Bunker Hill Monument, 49-50
Burlingame, Roger, 200
Barnum, Phineas T., 196
Beebe, Lucius, 216
Borglum, Gutzon, 174

C

Cabrillo National Monument, San Diego, Calif., 106
Calhoun, John C., 67
California Missions, 106
Cape Hatteras National Recreation Area, 62
Carmer, Carl, 156
Carver, George Washington, 143
Castle, Eugene W., 46
Catton, Bruce, 97, 120
Channing, W. E., 60
Charleston, S. C., 67
Charlottesville, Va., 87
Chastellux, Marquis de, 85
Chief Crazy Horse Monument, 20
Chief Tecumseh, 21
Churchill, Winston, 17, 25, 35
Cody, W. F., Memorial and Museum, Cody, Wyo., 167, 170
Collis, John Stewart, 56
Coloma, Calif., 107
Colter, John, 59
Commager, Henry Steele, 39, 185, 193
Conestoga Wagons, 101

239

DUE

	PRINTED IN U.S.A.